Intentional RELATIONSHIPS

A GUIDE TO DATING WITH PURPOSE

TOLU FABIYI

authorHOUSE®

AuthorHouse™ UK
1663 Liberty Drive
Bloomington, IN 47403 USA
www.authorhouse.co.uk
Phone: 0800.197.4150

Published by AuthorHouse   10/10/2018

ISBN: 978-1-5462-9715-4 (sc)
ISBN: 978-1-5462-9717-8 (hc)
ISBN: 978-1-5462-9716-1 (e)

For more information about this book, the author and additional products, programs and partnership opportunities, visit www.tolufabiyi.com

Print information available on the last page.

Unless otherwise indicated, all Scripture quotations are taken from the Holy Bible, New Living Translation, copyright ©1996, 2004, 2007 by Tyndale House Publishers, inc., Wheaton, Illinios 60189.

CONTENTS

Dedication vii

Acknowledgements...ix

A Welcome From Someone Who's Been There......................xi

Introduction xiii

Chapter 1   Her Story...1

Chapter 2   The Time And The Season 17

Chapter 3   The Gift Of Singleness (More Than Waiting) 27

Chapter 4   Defective Dating And Situationships 43

Chapter 5   Introducing Love 53

Chapter 6   Purpose Of Dating 65

Chapter 7   105 Questions To Be Asked When Dating With
             Purpose...73

Chapter 8   Principled Dating. How To Date (Intentionally)
             With A Purpose 83

Chapter 9   New Attitude..97

Chapter 10   While You Wait 107

Chapter 11   What Next? Trust In The Lord............................ 115

DEDICATION

This book is dedicated to God Almighty for blessing me with a gift and using me as an instrument to touch the lives of His people. To all the singles and dating who have shared their stories of confusion, struggles and heartbreak with me over the years, this book is for you. I also dedicate this book to all the young men and women who are single or in a relationship, looking to build intentional relationships and defy the myths of dating in today's world. My prayer is that this book will make your relationships more intentional and fruitful.

ACKNOWLEDGEMENTS

I would like to express my sincere gratitude to the many people who stood by me through this book; to all those who provided support, talked things over, read, wrote, offered comments and criticisms, allowed me to quote their experiences, tell their stories and remarks and assisted in the editing, proofreading and design, I really appreciate you all.

To my awesome fiancé (at the time of writing this book) Dr. Adedeji Fabiyi, now my husband: God bless you abundantly for your unending support, countless ideas, contacts, feedbacks, taking all my tears, worries, struggles, complaints and most of all, for standing with me as we birth the work of God. I can't tell you how much I love you. You are simply the best. Thank you for being intentional in our relationship. Sending you lots of love and kisses.

A WELCOME FROM SOMEONE WHO'S BEEN THERE

Dear Friend,

Do you ever wish relationships came with warning signs that would light up bright in your face and tell you when you need to take your leave? Do you ever wish relationships came with a manual, rules and regulations, roles and responsibilities suitable for the opposite sex etc.?? Well, sometimes I do and other times I don't. Especially as I listen to the stories and experiences of male and female friends, friends of their friends, and even strangers, it often makes me wish there was set principles or procedures on how to date; just so both parties can avoid some unnecessary drama in life.

I had my share of the drama-filled life as well. I didn't really care for principles, order, or any of such, I just wanted to love and be loved. *That should be simple enough*, I thought. Boy was I wrong. I've made my companion everything from ups and downs, a heavy heart, tears in my eyes as I retire to bed, confusion, and so many others.

I am still a work in progress, still learning. But now I know better than what I knew when my relationship life was filled with unwanted drama. For this, I am grateful to God for giving me a better understanding of this whole relationship saga.

Perhaps you are skimming this book, convinced that you don't have time to read it, but you want to make a difference in your relationship life. You want to date intentionally and love on purpose. Well, KNOWLEDGE IS POWER. What you don't know, you don't know, but what you do know is what you can do something about. So, I encourage you to turn every page carefully, so you don't miss out on the power you need.

So, if you are single, in a relationship, heartbroken, engaged, and newly married or still trying to figure out this loving, dating and relationship business, let's walk together. The following pages will make you understand that we all have our stories, that you are not alone, and most importantly, help you understand singleness, love, and being intentional about your relationships.

INTRODUCTION

"The best way to ensure you achieve the greatest satisfaction out of life is to behave intentionally."
— Deborah Day, BE HAPPY NOW!

I stood and waited on the platform at the train station for ten minutes. The notice on the dispatch board was that the train kept being delayed due to engineering works. I was in a hurry, yet I found myself still standing and waiting for twenty more minutes. Then I thought to myself; I am wasting lots of time waiting for this train, I need to find an alternative route to get to where I need to be. I remembered I had passed by a bus stop on my way to the train station and immediately turned around to head for it. Five minutes later, with a few other faces, I had sighted at the train station, we all stood to wait for the bus. Thankfully I saw a bus approaching. I flagged it down, got onto it, touched my oyster card and quickly found a nice and comfortable seat to rest my tired self, having been waiting long enough already. A few minutes later, the bus stopped to pick a couple of passengers at another stop and soon headed to its destination. Not long after, I noticed the passengers on the bus became rowdy; they made a lot of noise and were out of control. I was puzzled.

Confused, I kept looking to the older lady sat next to me if she noticed what was going on and if she was even bothered or disturbed about this, but to my amazement, every time I stole a glance at her she smiled warmly at me. I thought to myself at this time of the day, the bus should not be rowdy, or did I get onto the wrong bus or something. I then started to imagine what my life would have been if I had been more patient in waiting for the overdue train at the station. I wondered if I happened to have come out of my house at the wrong time that day and what in the world was going on.

There was just a lot of noise, and the bus driver was not at all bothered. He just kept driving and stopping where necessary just as his job description stated. The journey had lasted for about thirty minutes, and it became unbearable, I figured I must have gotten onto the wrong bus so as soon as the driver pulled up at the next stop, I alighted. I watched the bus drive away from where I stood, trying to regain some peace of mind then it hit me that the area where I stood was not one I was familiar with; I did not know where I was. So, I asked myself, how can I possibly get to where I need to be from here?

Life has a way of taking you on journeys you never intended to embark on or on journeys you never end up understanding. As a young man or woman, we carry so many concerns about life on our shoulders and no doubt one of the greatest concerns is love and the fear of being alone. Being single or in a relationship is such a favourite topic among the youths of today. In this day and age, it is almost impossible to speak to a young boy or girl, man or woman about the topic of relationship with the opposite sex and not end up having a mouth and heart full of conversations.

A lot of people have stopped waiting on being single or on the purposeful relationship train to arrive. Perhaps they thought it would never arrive and decided to find another means to get to their destination faster, only to realise they got on the wrong bus and then they have to alight from the bus and map out another journey plan. They say there is no point in remaining single when you can go out there and date. No, I say there is a point to staying single if there is no purpose to your dating. If a purpose does not exist, abuse will inevitably become the order of the day. It will only be a cycle of unfortunate circumstances if purpose and intentionality are removed from the equation.

Today's concept of dating is sadly very misleading. So, they - the world, tell us, in order not to be left behind, start casting a vision for your marriage early enough. Unfortunately, whether the image is cast early or late, you find that books like this become necessary because there remains a lot of mind juggling singles who wonder if their perfect partner train will ever arrive, if it is permanently delayed or if it has even been cancelled. They give up on waiting to take a replacement service, and that makes their journey much.

After several years of waiting on God's promise to be fulfilled, Sarah sat down one day, and after much thought, she came up with an alternative plan which she presented to her husband, Abraham. He accepted this plan. Obviously tired of being in her state of despair, she gave her house maid Hagar to her husband in hopes of getting a child out of this arrangement. How mistaken she was. When God is leading you in a particular direction with your journey all mapped out, carving any contrary alternative route can only be borne out of impatience, doubt or unbelief.

Just like Sarah, many people have come up with alternatives to dating that have landed them in unplanned destinations. It is usually when we can no longer wait, or we are tired of waiting on something or someone that we come up with our alternatives. In most cases, these alternatives only chart a new and possibly longer course for you. Why not keep waiting.

Waiting on purpose or waiting intentionally is never the easiest thing to do. Nobody wants to wait. We all want things fast and now. Likewise dating intentionally is never the easiest thing to do. However, it is the most beneficial thing to do if you want to get it right. Imagine a life of you and your partner loving each other on purpose. Heavenly. This would be different from when one party is trying to love on purpose, and the other party just chooses to love when they can. If I said, this book would give you a structured guide on how to get into a relationship, get married and stay married forever that would be a lie. I have come to the understanding that doing things in life without purpose can be frustrating; it leaves you asking so many questions, it leaves you doubting yourself, your values and your worth as an individual. On the other hand, when you do things with purpose, there is a sense of acceptance and sometimes fulfillment. Growing up, I did a lot of things without purpose, more so because the friends I had at the time did the same thing. We cared less, it was what we wanted to do at the time, so we did it, regardless of whether it was right or wrong or purposeful or not and intentional or not. We did it anyway.

Standing at the bus stop where the bus left me made me question my actions and my attitude. I realised I had quickly jumped from one option to the other like most of us jump from one season of our lives to another season without giving much thought to anything. I asked myself questions like what was I doing at the bus stop? How did I get here? And how would I get to where I need to be in time? I started looking around for locals I could speak to who could direct me in the right way so I could plan my journey again. It was evident to me that I would not be able to figure it out myself nor did I intend on making the same mistake again. I was sure I needed help, so I sought help. Many of us have made terrible, unspeakable errors in the name of being in a relationship or dating or loving. We have dated for the sake of dating, for fear of remaining single for the rest of our lives, because we wanted companionship, because we desperately wanted to fill a void or vacuum in our lives, because of something we knew we were going to get out of that relationship, and our hearts have been broken several times but yet we refuse to admit and accept that the way we have been doing things need to change. It is impossible to keep doing the same thing repeatedly and expect to achieve a different result. Chances are you would keep getting the same results just in a variety of ways. It is time to try a different routine. It is time to try something new. It is time to live intentionally and date with purpose.

As I embarked on my journey to where I had to be, I kept asking questions along the way to enable me to get a clearer picture and understanding of my journey. So, I would ask locals on the way how do I get to Highgate station from here? Do I take a left or right? How many streets do I need to count? Does this bus go to Hanwell? What's the colour of the building I should look out for? If I did not ask questions, I was guaranteed to be frustrated on my clueless journey as well as waste precious time. Likewise, one important principle about dating with purpose is asking questions. If you do not ask questions, you would be making frustrating assumptions that you and your significant other are walking the same path which could be disastrous. During my secondary school, college and university days, I would ask questions in class, not to seem like I wanted to be noticed or like I knew it all but just to be sure I had a better understanding of the subject matter. Even at work, you ask questions when your supervisor or line manager assigns a task to you or gives you instructions you have to follow up on. It is mandatory for you to ask questions in other to have a sense of certainty with what you are dealing with.

The dating scene is now a roller coaster. Nobody wants to be single, everybody wants to date and be in a relationship, but not many people want to do this intentionally. Dating for the sake of dating is simply chaotic. It means you probably do not have the right understanding of some of the different seasons in your life i.e. the season to be single, to be in a relationship and to be married. These seasons have specific roles they play in shaping our whole life, but if you rush through one season to get to the next, there is a high chance you will have missed out on the gifts, blessings and opportunities in the previous season.

As you would imagine, there is no specific chapter or verse of the Bible that tells us how to date or a specific chapter or verse that refers to the word dating or its procedure. What you find are usually stories and knowledge of singles and married, stories that bother on our hearts or bodies, our attitudes and our purpose. These stories have formed a biblical guideline on dating today.

If you want to explore a life of intentional living with issues that bother on love, dating and relationships, I encourage you to come along with me as we go through the chapters of this book sharing stories of people that have dated without purpose, discussing seasons of singleness, love, situation-ships, dating with purpose, waiting and trusting God regardless of your relationship status. Do not let impatience create alternatives for you.

REFLECTIONS

CHAPTER ONE

HER STORY

"I wondered what happened when you offered yourself to someone, and they opened you, only to discover you were not the gift they expected, and they had to smile and nod and say thank you all the same."

— Jodi Picoult, My Sister's Keeper

A lot of times you find that when you counsel or advice people to make the right decisions on dating, and learn from the examples or experiences of others, they say 'this cannot happen to me'. This is often true until it happens to them. In my very few years on earth, I have been approached by friends, colleagues and even friends of other friends on what I think about certain things in relationship and dating. Most people do not believe anything can happen to them until they find themselves right in the center of it. In most cases this would be because people probably did not pay attention to certain things that they ought to have paid attention to, or as they say, 'life just happened'. Either way, they end up right at the center of it.

Your desire to leave your present employment should not override the need to move the right way. There is a reputation you want to leave behind, as you would want to ensure that you maintain the necessary relationship with the right people and nothing stops you from securing another employment elsewhere. Likewise, your desire to graduate from singleness should never override the need to do it the right way and intentionally. Perfection is a word far from every individual, even though some may seem like they do have it all together. No one is perfect, we all make mistakes here and there, but in choosing a life partner, one must be intentional with extra care as errors in this area of our lives are always very costly.

In this chapter, I have shared stories of ladies who have had similar dating experiences, and I have equally sought their permission to publish these stories. Their real names and locations have been changed to protect their reputation and privacy. These stories are to help young singles decide for themselves if they ever want more out of dating or if they would rather just keep dating. This is also to encourage young singles to be more intentional in dating, not just dating for the fun of it and shamelessly giving away our bodies to people that have no regard for it or leaving soul ties with people that would only remain in the past. For instance, you know how you intentionally go online and search for job vacancies, how you deliberately call up recruitment agencies in case they have a role that would be suitable for you; or how you intentionally study hard; so that you can pass that exam and be done with college. Or get the professional qualification already? Yeah, it's time to date intentionally too. It's time to date with a purpose.

JUNE'S STORY

Her name is June. A beautiful, young, smart and sweet girl who had a plan for what her life was to look like but was just not sure how the road had panned out through the journey. She was filled with the passion for greatness and being selfless as she was there was no limiting her, but she had just left home to a foreign country and was only 17 years when her story began. Starting University with an open mind, ready for what life brings along and in making new friends, she met Jake.

Slim, tall, intelligent, career driven, well dressed, captivating smile, funny and appearing to be somewhat of a brown chocolate in skin colour, this was Jake, just the way she had always dreamt of 'him' when 'he' decided to show up. June and Jake quickly hit it off and became good friends, with no caution or thought given to the next steps after friendship, they became 'an item' and started dating.

As with love birds, things were sweet and rosy as they found common interests in human intelligence, till it was not so any longer. June had grown up in a Christian home where the tenets of purity and holiness were daily preached at home. Jake had equally grown up in a Christian home but was not quite sure of his stance on those Christian values he was taught, but instead he quickly developed a mind of his own; after all, he was growing to become a man. Jake and June always made dinner date plans, adventure plans, travel plans and so on but never had the chance to make a purposed dating plan for each other, till it was too late, till she had given herself to him time and time again.

Her story changed, she had just turned 18.

June had compromised her standards and values for a man who shared a different set of values from her. She had prayed that her first boyfriend should be her husband. It, however, was not looking like what she had dreamed of and she tried to settle. She became more concerned, and after bitter sweet ten months, she wanted to re-plan this whole relationship. Although they were still very much in the same book, Jake was however no longer on the same page. They were now on different pages because purpose had been thrown out of the window. She had opened up and given everything inside of her to a stranger who had no future or imminent plan to accommodate her in his life. She allowed Jake take everything she was before she met him. Now, she desperately wanted to plan. She had tried to imagine what life would have been if she had not given herself to Jake, if they had taken the time to plan their relationship, if only they were clearer on the purpose of their relationship, but this was only an image that caused more pain and regrets. Jake had a mind of his own and had no intentions to change and with June determined to revise her standards, they broke up.

He was her first.

Four years later, June met Jude. June had spent the last four years building her relationship with Christ, praying for a man after Gods' heart to find her, embracing her singleness and making the most of it. She was in her rightful place. Then Jude a total stranger came pulling down the walls she had built over the last four years. This was not evident to June until about a year later. A friend of June had introduced Jude (an acclaimed born-again Christian) to her and just like reliving the sins of old; they wasted no time in cultivating a friendship, skipped the hurdle in between and boarded the next available dating train at the station. Jude was ten years older than June; this was the first time she would date a much older guy. Her friends were not comfortable with the idea and tried to persuade her not to rush into the relationship, as men of such age already have a preconceived notion of how that want a lady to be and would do everything possible to make her that way.

She could care less and was somewhat convinced he was 'THE ONE' she had been praying about and was delighted at how quick God responded to her prayer with her prince finding her. She thought to herself, God was quick on this one. As such, she ignored the warnings.

Jude would always hold her hands in public and together they would agree in prayer always led by him. They would usually sit outdoors talking about how good God is and how children of God were to have lives filled with joy, laughter, happiness and blessings. This behavior alone blinded June to other things that were to come her way in the relationship. She could have lengthy conversations about God with Jude which she never really did with Jake. Jude was a loving man, what else could she have needed. Love is great they say, so it was for June and Jude, but little did they know that they both had no idea what love was about. They had an idea but not the actual understanding. They could not possibly love each other without knowing what love truly meant and without understanding the love of Christ.

They had immediately laid a foundation with the fruits of the flesh. Again, there was no purpose or end goal for the relationship, but they kept at it. They simply liked each other and decided to live like couples in love. However, time usually reveals secrets, and this was the case for them. They did everything a married couple would do in a marriage and much more to the extent that nothing was new under the sun anymore, till the sun stopped shining on them and dusk appeared.

Peace disappeared and June started having various dreams, revealing that Jude confessed to seeing other ladies while she was out of the country; that he was not really a man who feared God; that he would derail her from her dreams and visions; that he already had a plan on what would become of her if they got married and so on. She could not understand these dreams and did not speak to anyone about it. So, she tried to endure for a little longer.

She decided to stay in the hopes of working things out in the name of the love they had both carved out for each other. It became more difficult; the fire appeared to be hotter than ever with only June getting burnt. Jude was not affected. He had become uncaring, he could stay weeks without getting in touch with June and whenever she called he would say he was busy and could not talk. They no longer prayed together, they no longer shared moments together, they no longer communicated, they were simply different busy souls caged in a box designed by them, where neither knew what the other was doing.

June wanted more than just having to give herself away too cheaply and shamelessly; she wanted what she had been praying for four years ago before she got sidetracked and settled with Jude. She out rightly knew the solution, but this was different. Breaking away was difficult. After three years of investment, she had given all that was left of her body, soul and spirit to Jude. How does she take any of it back and leave? When the heat was at its hottest, she was weak and had no strength even to pray, she left. Added to the list of yet another failed attempt at loving and dating, he was her second.

Not too far off, just less than five months down the line, James an old friend who had been waiting patiently in line comes forward just after the fortunate breakaway and June became the very girl she dreaded so much. She no longer understood the difference between like, love and hate. It was all purposeless to her. It was now a recognised way of life for June. They had tried being just friends, but it was hard to adjust, so they just kept up with what they were doing. Giving themselves away without purpose, it was all fun and games.

It was okay to always give herself to every man she believed to 'love', and the men in return were constantly expectant of the already known and accepted way of life; till something changed. It was evident, they were not sure where they were nor where they were going, but they found freedom in what they were without a title because remaining title-less was better because too many things get involved once a title was placed on what they were. She did not want to lose this friendship (at least she thought they had one). It was okay being a friend with benefits. It appeared she was just trying to fill a void unconsciously.

It had become apparent that they were merely renting spaces in each other's heart and they both refused to be evicted. What she was doing during the past situation-ships, was leaving pieces of her heart, body, soul, spirit and her very being with the men who regarded her with little or nothing. She had no regard for herself and the temple that belonged to God. Again, it became apparent that she was more than what she had turned out to be and decided to take a break from dating. She left with a distorted heart. Added to the list again, he was her third.

Trapped between hurt and lowered expectations, life meant so much more to her than the absurd and shameless way she knew how to. She started asking questions, like what is the point of building memories that would last forever when they both know that they would only last temporarily together. She decided to try to make the conscious decision to be better. She went back to the drawing board to truly revise her standards, map out the boundaries and create a focus. Before all of this, there was a journey, she was going somewhere, there was a vision and a goal, she needed help, she wasn't about to make the same mistake again.

It became much clearer that she was a queen with Godly standards, precious values, firm boundaries and excellent principles, knowing not to let her heart away, knowing to guard her heart jealously for her King whenever he showed up. She realised she was more than what she thought she was.

Albeit, after three bouts of 'love' and 'situation-ships', she needed help.

It was time to live intentionally and date with a purpose.

LESSONS TO BE LEARNT

- **June had no understanding of the biblical love we ought to emulate.**
- **June had not allowed enough time during her friendships to know the type of men she was getting involved with.**
- **She had attached too much value to Jude's claim of being born again. Remember the bible says, *'By their fruits you shall know them'.* You cannot hide your true self for long; time will definitely reveal the real you.**
- **She did not seek wise counsel, neither did she ask relevant questions or pray fervently.**
- **Never totally disregard warnings of parents and friends.**
- **In a relationship if you are of a strong faith, it is advisable to have a partner with the same beliefs and values as yourself, if dissimilar; this would build a foundation for serious problems.**

TINA'S STORY

Tina was a young girl just starting law school when she met Jordan. She had met Jordan's older sister who then introduced her to her brother (a considerable much older man). Jordan was a well to do man, who had various businesses around the city and was doing well for himself. Tina had come from a home where her mother had to support her and her sisters in the absence of her father. She had grown to be a very strong woman knowing how to fend and take care of herself. She had some Christian values which she learnt while growing up, but with Jordan around, those values were sometimes abandoned deep down in a safe in her heart. This relationship wasn't necessarily for Christian values.

Things got heated quickly, and Tina and Jordan became an item. He regularly showered her with gifts and occasionally showered her with his presence. As things went on, Tina found that she would regularly visit him at home, spend quality time with him, cook for him and carry out the duties and serve the role of a wife, except that there was no ring on her finger and God had not sealed any relationship between them. She would hang out with him and his friends late at night, visit night clubs, restaurants and travel together. Sometimes, they would have heated arguments, not speak to each other for days because one was upset with the other and then eventually makeup and then carry on as if nothing happened. Every night they were together, they would both give themselves away cheaply to each other, failing to recognise the effect of their actions, they found comfort and solace in exploring each other's body. Tina had agreed to start this relationship because she knew Jordan's older sister and she needed a man old enough to take care of her needs, what she didn't know was that Jordan was not the man she needed.

One evening, during the regular visits and out of the blues, Jordan confessed to Tina that he had been married before. He explained that he was in the process of a divorce, from his wife who had cheated on him. Although they were no longer together, she already had three kids for him. This was shocking news to Tina; she almost thought it was some joke. But it was true. She was broken. She could not phantom that fact that there had been another woman in the position of a wife before her and her prince charming also had three kids already. She was mad at him; she confronted him, she thought he deceived her into falling in love with him by not telling her the truth earlier on in their relationship, called him names and threatened to end their relationship. This was too much to bear. She decided to take the time to put herself together.

Not for long, Tina was back, loving Jordan all over again. She had thought to herself that Jordan must love her to have told her his secret, after all, he and his ex-wife are divorced. There is no human without mistakes, neither is there anyone with perfection. She wasn't perfect either. She found a way to adjust to this new role of 'second wife' even before intentions were made known; she would always ask after the kids, find time to play, bond with them and show them, love, since they were now going to be under her care when she gets married to Jordan. Tina had hoped the storm was clear in the relationship, not until Jordan came visiting one night again.

He was all moody and didn't speak much until Tina forced out what she could not understand from his mouth. He told her he had met a lady a while ago and they had a 'one-night stand', she got pregnant and just gave birth to a set of twins for him. He said he had to tell Tina face to face as opposed to over the phone. This is the second woman and now with a set of twins for him. Tina was furious and immediately sent Jordan out of her apartment that night. She could not believe what she had heard; she could not believe it was true, she could not believe this was happening to her; it had to be a joke. It appeared like Jordan now had a trend of sleeping with women with no purpose but leaving his seed to grow inside of them. Could this be a thing of choice or circumstance for Jordan, she thought to herself. She had been told that marriage is a place where two people come with different baggage's, so just find the one who would help you unpack your baggage or one which you are willing to help carry his or her baggage. This was too much a baggage for her alone to bear.

Not understanding what love is, can be very dangerous. After so many tears, thinking, pacing about and days of doing nothing, she placed a call to him saying she still loved him and would stand by him to support him through it all. She wanted to be the ride or die woman in his life. At that moment in her life she desperately wanted companionship and was afraid of being alone, not loved by any, she wanted this love to last. She wanted to stick it till the end. What is love if you don't fight for it, so she thought.

After three years, one night, Tina and Jordan had their usual chat before going to bed. One thing led to another and Tina passed a comment about his manner of dressing and the rest of the conversation was what resulted to the end of the relationship. The comment did not sit well with Jordan as he literarily striped Tina off her entire self. He insulted her image, her individuality, her career choice and her attitude. He stated that she was a careless speaker and he had only been managing her all this while in the relationship. Tina was dumb shocked; she could not believe her ears again, he had just stripped her off without any mercy. This was it for her. She then remembered her mother's warnings that Jordan was not the man for her and would only make life difficult for her. She then knew that this was certainly not the man she was going to marry. She was willing to help him carry his baggage, but he wasn't ready to let go of the baggage, it had become the life he was used to. This time, she was really broken. She took her time to evaluate the years spent with Jordan and decided that she could be better than this. It was time to really seek the face of God for a man that would love her as Christ loved the church. No lies, no secrets, no disrespects and no dead ends. She wanted more than anything else, a purposeful relationship with a purposeful man.

LESSONS TO BE LEARNT

- Tina was desperate for a relationship because she needed someone to satisfy her needs. Had she taken her time, she would have probably known Jordan a little well enough to affirm whether or not she should venture into the relationship.
- Intentionally seek Gods face before dating. There is no need to rush if you don't want to end up rushing out.
- In dating, it is important to identify the flaws of your intended spouse that you can cope with and those you cannot tolerate. It is better to have a broken relationship than a broken marriage. Be intentional in identification.
- Do not bend your rules for any reason except you feel it's not that important to you or it is in accordance with the purpose of God for your life.
- Do not forsake the instructions of your parents. Chances are you may not understand your parents' view of the relationship because love and romance may be clouding your judgment.
- Old habits, die hard.
- Mutual respect is very vital for the success of any relationship.

∞

MARIAM'S STORY

Mariam spent four years of her life with George and looking back now; it really wasn't the most purposeful years of their relationship. They had met when they newly started university together; they quickly became friends and without hesitation became an item. Amongst a few friends, they were regarded as the best couple in school. It wasn't a hidden relationship as such. Mariam had come from a more Westernised

Muslim background, but her parents had a very strong view on keeping the culture closer to home. They wanted their daughter to marry a someone from the same religious faith. Mariam rather developed her own views on the kind of man she was interested in when she met George. He was from a different African country from Mariam and had only just moved to The United States of America for his studies. He was brought up in a religious home which strictly condemns all forms of ungodliness. Being a man, he was also quick to develop his own views on the kind of woman he wanted. Their love grew stronger over the first two years of University with Mariam occasionally attending church services with George. Their religious ideas and values were different, but that was not a bother as the relationship was not based on that but more on the love they shared with each other.

Into the third year of the relationship, it began to dawn on Mariam that George was a different person. He started keeping very late nights with his boys, started seeing other ladies and wanted to be in control of who Mariam could see and not see. He became in charge, always scaring away other guys who had the slightest interest in Mariam. He knew he couldn't have her for life but was not willing to let go of her just yet. He was eating his cake and having it at the same time. Mariam confronted him on several occasions, and he would usually apologise, and they quickly returned to loving each other again. Mariam would cook, clean, care and even give herself to George whenever the need arose. She felt dirty, but she was not one to voice out problems to people. She worked best by keeping things secret which left most of her friends in a guessing game. She knew she could not tell her parents about this relationship, but she kept at it. Her friends wondered why she was hurting herself and leaving deeper wounds in her heart because of the relationship. Any friend that dared to counsel Mariam from the obvious was her enemy. She would agree with the friend saying she would end things and the next minute she increases her love dose by 100% while ignoring the friend. She was his confidant, he was her confidant, and they had grown to know much about each other that other friends did not know. But this was not enough; they were not exactly compatible in other areas that mattered most to them.

During the fourth year of their relationship which was the final year of university, they had a big fight and were not speaking to each other. I guess it was beginning to get clear that this relationship was just to last the time of university. After their university exams, the results showed that George failed the course and had to re-sit the exams to be given a better grade, while Mariam had to graduate with the lowest grade available at the school. They were intelligent science students, but the unintentional and purposeless relationship had affected their journey through university. How do they explain this to their parents? Should they be ashamed of each other, I mean it was love, and no one should regret loving anyone. Mariam left when the University was over and never to hear from George again. George on the other hand, realising he was fast becoming a man, had to make his results right because he knew he needed them. He remained in University, had his re-sit exams and was awarded a better grade than what he was initially granted. He returned home, never to hear from Mariam again.

They had both given four years of their lives to each other for nothing. Love shared purposely is better enjoyed. There was no direction and no intention in their relationship. From the onset, they both knew they could not get married due to religious differences, but they still endured four years of sharing each other's body, soul and spirit all to tear it down years later. George was not new in the dating game, but for Mariam, he was her first long term relationship. Her friends believed this experience, crushed her on the inside. It had taken a while before she was able to lift her head up out of the maze. The purpose was absent in the four years they spent together.

LESSONS TO BE LEARNT

- It is advisable for your partner to have the same religious beliefs as you, otherwise there would be serious problems if you go ahead to marry such person.
- Mariam ignored counsels of friends which was a grave mistake.
- If you cannot tell your parents about your relationship, this alone in most cases is a sign that you are doing something wrong.
- In making the choice of a life partner, the questions of compatibility and communication must arise. If these questions are not answered satisfactorily, it is a danger signal.
- Do not be carried away by the gifts, love and affection showered by people. Try not to lose focus during love, always keep your heart in check.

REFLECTIONS

CHAPTER TWO

THE TIME AND THE SEASON

There is a time for everything and a season for every activity under heaven..."

— Ecclesiastes 3:1

Time is a precious commodity.

Time is everything.

For everything in life, under the sun, there is a time and a season. How beautiful and comforting is it, knowing that there is a designated time for things to happen in life.

With my father being a pastor, my parents were somewhat regarded as marriage counsellors in church. As you would imagine, everyone brought their stories and situations on singleness, being in a relationship, being married or divorced, to marriage counselors. As a result of hearing a lot of these stories, my parents would daily counsel us at home on the struggles people face in this thing called relationship and how we needed to avoid such issues by not jumping ahead of our seasons.

One evening, I had just retired home from work, exhausted, my bed was the next calling, but that was the perfect time for another counselling session from my parents. Half asleep I paid attention to the story of a young lady who started dating at a very early age and after several dates; she ended up getting married to one of them. She was only 18, and he was 20. Their first two years in marriage was heaven on earth; this was new to them, so they enjoyed every bit of the experience by loving each other in every way possible. Approaching the third year of their marriage tiredness set in and they both could not give as much as they thought they would have been able to give. She wanted children, but he was kind enough to explain to her that he did not want any child.

Years went by, and they grew further apart, they both seemed disinterested in the things of each other, and it appeared as if they were lodgers in the same house. She did not understand if she had suddenly changed or if her husband had suddenly changed, but it was certain something had changed. Ten years later, lodging with someone you don't really care about anymore became the problem. Everything this lady did became an abomination to her husband. It was as if she could no longer do anything right. They both started experiencing traits about themselves that they never knew about ten years ago.

Things began to become clumsy in the house with no one wanting to discuss divorce because of the preconceived notion of society on divorce. It was just two of them with no children, so it was an easy decision for her husband. He left to start a new life in another country. How did she find out? Well, he sent her a postcard. She was utterly shocked. She could not believe what her life had turned out to be at the age of 30. She was all alone with no husband, no children and family had become distant due to her husband's regulations, she thought of suicide. I had managed to put sleep on hold and was well awake at this point. She wanted to take her own life because her married season was over and there was no life after that season for her. So she thought.

Although this book is not about staying or being married, the lady's story is only a pointer to the fact that there is a season for everything in life. As a young lady, the season of being in a relationship and getting married should not be the top of your list just yet. Instead of jumping ahead of yourself and missing out on important seasons of your life, take a back seat and enjoy your seasons without rush. It is most likely that they both did not take time to go through their single seasons before embarking on the marriage season. Things that would have been discovered and dealt with were not discovered until the next season but unfortunately were never dealt with. Their previous season may have better prepared them for the battles in the next season. This is not to say that only those who go through seasons of singleness will be the best at their marriage season. No. Every season has its challenges and things to overcome, but there are also many joys and victories to be won if only we go through the seasons intentionally.

Most of us will not remain single forever, or for our entire lives and as such, our present circumstance whether single or married is to be viewed as a season in our lives, differently timed for every individual. Paul in the Bible gives a nice outline for the proper attitude towards singleness in *1 Corinthians 7* which will be further discussed at length in chapter four of this book. This chapter for emphasis sake is simply to introduce you to the different times and seasons of one's life. Once you are aware of this, you will no doubt live life more intentionally, embracing and accepting every moment.

Let's start with God's timing. When you know that a time has been set for you for a specific thing to happen, you would typically anticipate that thing and prepare for it. This is the right attitude to have knowing that God has a set time for you to be in a relationship or for you to get married. Have you ever tried to pray for Grace to always stay patient and trust in His timing? Have you ever tried to trust that He will do it because He said He will? Remember that God always says He will do it, but he just never puts a time frame on it. It would have been a lot easier if we knew His timing, but then we would have no need for faith anymore. We would no longer need to have faith to stay in peace and trust in His timing.

The Bible says, the vision is for an appointed time *(Habakkuk 2:3)* and the appointed time, no doubt, is the right time. Only God can see the big, bigger and biggest picture of our lives; He knows what and who we need and how and when it needs to show up. He knows what will happen in the long run and what our lives would be like, which is why He shuts certain doors early enough in our lives. If it has not been done yet, instead of being worried or frustrated, just trust Gods timing, because if it is already in God's plan for you, then you will have it at the appointed time. Remember, it is only through Faith and Patience that we will inherit the promises of God *(Hebrews 6:12)*. It's easy to have faith, but we also need to have patience. You not only believe that you will have a spouse, but you also intentionally choose to trust His timing as to when the spouse will appear.

Just like a pregnant mother, during the pregnancy she may experience some pain, discomfort and tiredness; she may be uncomfortable and might want the baby out before the due time. It's no news that babies are generally to be delivered after nine months of pregnancy, so it is safe to say the appointed time for a baby to be born would be when the time has been properly served in the womb. Therefore, since it is not the right time for the child to leave the womb, anything done to bring the baby out of the womb long before its appointed time could lead to several mishaps. Imagine what could happen if the child came out long before its due or appointed time. So also, are the seasons of our lives and the things we ask for from God. Sometimes we get easily carried away, and we want to help God in making things quicker. When we take time in our hands, and we force things to happen outside of God's timing, or we force our seasons to change prematurely, we will be obligated to take care of that thing ourselves.

Remember Ishmael; it was difficult for Sarah and Abraham to raise him as a child because that was not God's plan for them. They decided to help God out by an alternative means. Nonetheless, at the set time, God gave them Isaac, the child God intended for them. Likewise, in our dating lives, if we let go of Ishmael, our Isaac will show up. God has it all figured out, just trust Him. Don't go around birthing and settling for Ishmael when God has Isaac in store for you. If you let God do it in his timing, you'll find God's peace in it. So, you do not have to force doors to open for yourself when you can keep your time in God's hands and let God open that door for you.

William J. Bennett in "THE BOOK OF VIRTUES" tells a fascinating story called "The Magic Thread". This was a story of a boy named Peter, strong and able, yet flawed by an attitude of impatience. He was always dreaming about the future and was always dissatisfied with his present condition.

One day, while wandering in the forest, Peter meets a strange old woman who gives him a most tantalising opportunity – the chance to skip the dull, mundane moments of life. She hands Peter a silver ball from which a tiny gold thread protrudes. "This is your life thread" the woman explained. "Do not touch it and time will pass normally. But if you wish time to pass more quickly, you have only to pull the thread a little way an hour will pass like a second. But I warn you, once the thread has been pulled out, it cannot be pushed back on again.

For an impatient boy, this magical thread seemed to be the answer to all of Peter's problems. It is what he had always wanted; he takes the ball and runs home.

The following day in school, Peter has his first opportunity to put the silver ball to use by pulling some thread. The lesson is dragging, and the teacher scolds Peter for not concentrating. Peter fingers the silver ball and gives the thread a slight tug. Suddenly the teacher dismisses the class and Peter is free to leave school. He is overjoyed! How easy his life will now be? From this moment, Peter begins to pull the thread a little every day.

But soon, Peter begins to use the magic thread to rush and skip through larger portions of his life. Why waste time pulling just a little thread every day when he can pull it hard and complete school altogether? He does so and finds himself out of school and apprenticed in a trade. Peter uses the same technique to rush through his engagement to his sweetheart. He could not bear to wait months to marry her, so he used the gold thread to hasten the arrival of his wedding day. Peter continues this pattern throughout his life. When hard, trying times come, he escapes them with his magic thread. When the baby cries at night, when he faces financial struggles, when he wishes his children to be launched in careers of their own, Peter pulls the magic thread and bypasses the discomfort of the moment.

But sadly, when it comes to the end of his life, Peter realises the emptiness of such an existence. By allowing impatience and discontentment to rule him, Peter has robbed himself of life's richest moments, memories and seasons. With only the grave to look forward to, Peter deeply regrets having to use the magic thread.

In introducing this story, the author Mr. Bennett comments that "Too often, people want what they want or what they think they want right now. The irony of their impatience is that only by learning to wait and by a willingness to accept every season as it comes (the bad and the good), do we usually attain those things that are truly worthwhile".

Thankfully, while we do not possess the magic gold thread to rush us through life, we can however still develop wrong attitudes that have a similar effect. God wants us to appreciate the gifts of the present season of our lives. He wants us to learn the patience and trust necessary in every season he gives to us, remembering that the happenings of one season thrives on the next season.

In today's world, we are not readily acceptable of the concept of delayed gratification. Culture and social media has taught us that if something is good, we should seek to enjoy it immediately. So, we do best by escaping the confines of time, speeding up our pace and doing whatever it takes to beat the clock. This attitude is what we now practice in our dating lives. One reason why we have adopted this immediate gratification mentality is that we have lost sight of what is important – the biblical principle of time and seasons *Ecclesiastes 3:1-8*. It reads as follows:

> "Everything that happens in this world happens at the time God chooses
> A right time for birth and another for death,
> A right time to plant and another to reap,
> A right time to kill and another to heal,
> A right time to destroy and another to construct,
> A right time to cry and another to laugh,
> A right time to lament and another to cheer,
> A right time to make love and another to abstain,
> A right time to embrace and another to part,
> A right time to search and another to count your losses,
> A right time to hold on and another to let go,
> A right time to rip out and another to mend,
> A right time to shut up and another to speak up,
> A right time to love and another to hate,
> A right time to wage war and another to make peace".

Remember the story of Joseph in the book of Genesis. There was a time for him to be in prison and an appointed time for his release. The Bible makes us understand that after Joseph interpreted the Chief Butler's dream in prison and he was subsequently released, the Chief Butler forgot about him for two years. Now, it is important to note that if Joseph had been remembered earlier, his story would have been different as there would have been no dream for him to interpret at the time, he would not become a ruler at the time he did, and God's name would not be glorified the way God wanted it. So, God had an appointed time for Joseph's release. The time that would glorify his name and everyone would acknowledge and testify that God really was with Joseph. His appointed time was when Pharaoh dreamt. God's timing for Joseph was perfect.

Just as spring's role is different from fall, so also each of the seasons of our lives have different emphasis, focus and beauty. One is not better than the other as each season yields its own fruits and unique treasures. We cannot skip ahead to experience the riches of another season any more than a farmer can push the spring. Each season builds on the one before it. There is something in your present season that would be needed in and for your next season. Don't try to jump seasons instead try to enjoy every part of every season.

Seasons of our lives, come with different experiences. Just because something is good, doesn't mean we should experience it right now, we must remember that the right thing at the wrong time is still the wrong thing regardless. Even the bible says, "all things are good, but not all things are beneficial" (*1 Corinthians 10:23*). Looking at this, considering the season you find yourself; obviously, sex alone will be a pleasant experience but the right season where it will be beneficial is during marriage, not when indulged outside of marriage.

Likewise, if I told you I wanted to buy some oranges and you knew oranges were in season, you would not have a problem with that. However, if I told you I wanted to buy some mangoes and you know too well that mangoes are currently not in season; my move to go looking for mangoes will sound strange and absurd to you. This means you do not need to go shopping for what is not in season. This is because you will most likely not find what you are looking for, or you simply end up with something that looks like a mango. God has a perfect plan for your life. It is possible that that plan includes marriage and he has the right person somewhere for you. You may not know this person, you may have never set your face on this person, you may have never even travelled to where he or she lives, but when the season is right, you will meet the person. However, if you spend your entire time and energy trying to hunt this person down, you might end up in circles, at a dead end or with the wrong person. If, however, you find this person in the wrong season of your life, whatever relationship is nurtured between you and the person will be premature.

Let's do our future spouses a favour and stop shopping around prematurely.

Ask yourself these questions:

- Am I on my timing or God's timing?
- Am I trying to help God in abridging the time?
- Am I concentrating on only pleasing my creator?
- Am I using this season of my life for God?
- Am I using this season just to pursue a romantic relationship with someone by dating?
- Could I possibly be throwing away the gift of singleness?
- Am I fulfilling purpose in my current season?

Do you know women of God in ministry that are not married, still single? Yes. I still wonder at the fact that the area of life that the world would have seen to be the greatest cause of pain has become the most powerful part of their ministry. Honestly and genuinely, if we release our desires and become more focused on trusting God's timing and making the most of the seasons we are in, God can transform our distress and disappointment into present joy that will remain undisturbed, no matter how long it takes for the fruit we want to come into full bloom.

The funny thing about seasons is that they may feel as if they will go on and on and on till eternity. Yes, sometimes we ask ourselves, will I be single forever especially when that present season is not the most favourite of seasons. It is however inevitable. This too shall pass. If you have faith and exercise patience, you will inherit the promises of God. Likewise, if you remain faithful to embrace your season and plant the right seed, your moment of harvest will surely come. And when it does, it will yield your heart desires.

REFLECTIONS

CHAPTER THREE

THE GIFT OF SINGLENESS (MORE THAN WAITING)

"A busy, vibrant, goal-oriented woman is so much more attractive than a woman who waits around for a man to validate her existence."
— Mandy Hale, The Single Woman: Life, Love, and a Dash of Sass

"One of the greatest advantages of singleness is the potential for greater focus on Christ and accomplishing work for Him."
— Elizabeth George, Breaking the Worry Habit... Forever!: God's Plan for Lasting Peace of Mind

This was a perplexing phrase for me to accept when my close friend came running to me saying she has a gift from God. I wondered what the gift could be, a husband? A car? or a house perhaps? To my surprise it was singleness. I could not understand it. The pastor had succeeded in making people see a different side of singleness. I was eager to hear the sermon; I wanted to understand how singleness could be a gift, I would have thought it was just a normal part of life we all have to go through. As much as it was, it was also a gift. That was the different part I was made to understand.

To all the single ladies out there, yes ladies singleness is not a sin. Singleness is a gift. Singleness is a privilege. Singleness is part of the process. Singleness is only a phase differently timed for every individual. Contrary to what the world teaches now and what the churches do not teach, not every individual is called to marriage and this was seen in the book of Matthew as will be discussed later in this chapter.

Let's take this study from the beginning of creation. Before any and everything present here on earth now, there was God. Now the book of Genesis makes us understand that God decided to make man in his own image and likeness. So, God made a 'single' person who happened to be a man named Adam. Adam as a single person had a relationship with God; he had the power to name all the living creatures that moved on the surface of the earth.

Now the truth about this part of the Bible is that Adam must have been content being single. His relationship with God was enough for him; it was him and God all the way. Imagine that beauty, with you and God and a bunch of other beautiful and loving creatures. That would be bliss. Now, when God saw everything he had created and decided that it was not good for man to be alone, it was God's choice to make Adam a helpmate. God and Adam had a relationship. It was God's choice as to when another human being should be created to be a partner or helpmate to Adam. It was not Adams choice. It was God's choice. Now, God did not just simply create Eve out of another dust of the earth nor did he just call Eve into being, but God caused Adam to fall into a deep sleep while He (God) created Even out of Adams' rib. This is the message right here. Adam must have woken up from the deep sleep to see a woman (created from man) called Eve, created by God. But while he was asleep it is safe to say that God created Eve and knew who she was, had a relationship with her before Adam woke up to see her as a woman, a helpmate for him.

In today's world, we get to a particular stage in our lives, and we tell God, yeah it is time, I need a spouse, I have achieved so many things in my life, I need a mate to share the rest of my life with. We forget that the necessity of a spouse is God's choice. We forget that both Adam and Eve had their separate individual relationships with God before they even knew or had relationships with each other. It is important for us in today's world to seek a deeper and closer relationship with God, being able to say that God is enough for us genuinely. Knowing that God is sufficient for you, enables you in your walk with God to get into that phase where He allows to match with you that someone special who already has an existing relationship with Him, after all, it was God himself that said: "It is not good for man to be alone".

THE GIFT

Singleness is the foundation of all relationships. Singleness is the foundation of the first building block of society, not marriage as both individuals are first single before coming together in marriage. In other words, before there were two, three, four, five, six, seven, eight, nine, ten, etc. individuals, there was one single individual. From the explanation above, one can categorically say that singleness is God's original foundation.

In the beginning it was Adam alone before Adam and Eve together. We find three types of singleness in *Matthew 19 vs. 1-12* where Jesus had a discussion with the Pharisees about divorce and marriage. The Pharisees wanted to know if a man can divorce his wife for any reason as being observed by the world today. Jesus responded by explaining that when a man leaves his father and mother to join his wife, the two are then united into one. He continued by saying that divorce was not God's original intended idea but unless a wife has been unfaithful or committed adultery can divorce be permitted. Any other reason other than adultery is not permitted. This appeared to be a huge concern to the disciples as they then said to Jesus, 'maybe is it then better not to marry'. Jesus then replied speaking of three types of singleness: first, genetic – 'they were born that way' (v.12a) and 'never give marriage a thought' (MSG). Second, there is involuntary singleness (v.12b) – those who 'never get asked – or accepted' (MSG). Third, there is voluntary singleness – those who 'decide not to get married for Kingdom reasons' (v.12c, MSG). In other words, singleness can be temporary or permanent.

Paul in discussing this further in *1 Corinthians 7*, talks about the difference between being single and being married. Paul's teaching dwells at length on the topic singleness. Paul advocates that singleness is a privilege and not a punishment, and he encourages us to look upon singleness as a gift. A gift in the sense that we can use our single life to appreciate and take on many opportunities to develop ourselves and enhance the kingdom of God daily without the distractions that come with marriage. Yes, contrary to what social media teaches, some distractions come with being married. What do you do with a gift? You say thank you, you unwrap it and discover its charm or usefulness and you embrace its value and take complete ownership of it. People would usually not resent a gift. Therefore, if we can identify singleness as a gift from God, we would not resent it so much rather; we would take ownership of it and make the best of our singleness.

From Paul's teaching, he does not seem to condemn marriage as such but rather counsels us to remain unmarried just as he was, accepting whatever situation the Lord has us in. He counselled further that if you do get married, it is not a sin; however, his teachings are only to spare us of the additional problems and possible distractions that come with marriage because you do not need to be married to fulfil God's need and purpose in your life. Paul's teachings are not necessarily to place restrictions on us but to help us do whatever will help us serve the Lord best with as few distractions as possible. He ends his teaching by stating that 'the person who marries does well, and the person who does not marry, does even better'. Thus, one can agree as much as being married is a blessing, singleness also comes with its own share of blessings and is a state to be pursued and not avoided.

Now, not every individual is called to the ministry of marriage hence why Paul calls singleness a privilege. Not forgetting that Marriage is an institution established by God, some are called to marry while others are called to remain single for reasons stated in *Matthew 19* as identified above. Many believers in the world now are refusing God's gift of singleness, pouting and petulantly complaining that they would much rather have been graced with the gift of marriage.

Christopher Ash summarises it this way: "I know which 'gift' I have a simple test: if I am married, I have the gift of marriage; if I am not married, I have the gift of being unmarried." That leaves us with an important implication and application: "My circumstances are God's gracious gifts to me, and I am to learn to accept them from His hand as such." This is indeed the truth.

God does not leave any of his people without a gift. If you are currently single, you have no reason to think you have been ignored or forgotten when God was giving out gifts. No, you should view your current or present circumstance as God's gift to you, just as marriage will be your gift if and when God brings you a spouse. While you ought to consider deliberately remaining single *(see 1 Corinthians 7:7, 25-40)* in your present season, you are still free before God to desire marriage, to pray for it, and to pursue it intentionally.

It is crucial to understand that God's gift provides you with a unique ability and responsibility to serve and honour him. Tim Keller points out that when Paul speaks of "gifts", he refers to "an ability God gives to build others up." "The single calling which Paul speaks of is neither a condition without a struggle nor on the other hand an experience of misery. It is fruitfulness in life and ministry through the single state. When you have this gift, there may indeed be struggles, but the main thing is that God is helping you grow spiritually and be fruitful in the lives of others despite them."

God gives good gifts. To some, he graciously gives the gift of marriage and all the abilities and responsibilities that attend it. To others, he graciously gives the gift of singleness and all its capabilities and responsibilities. Some experience only the gift of singleness. Some experience a long gift of singleness followed by a short gift of marriage. Whether gifted with singleness or marriage, both opportunities are to be used for fruitfulness in life and ministry.

To be single, to be in a relationship or to be married requires love as a Christian. Now, if you are still in your single phase, this should be something you desire to understand before getting into any relationship. It has been said that one who does not love the Lord or his or herself, cannot possibly show love to another. This is the truth.

HOW TO EMBRACE YOUR SINGLENESS

1. <u>**Find full and unconditional love in Jesus first:**</u>

The longing to be fully known and fully loved is only fulfilled through a real relationship with Christ. No person can love us better than Him. He knows every secret sin, every glaring fault, and if we are hidden in him by faith, we are covered by his precious blood. We are forgiven, free, and loved. It is important to treasure this truth and trust that he can and will be enough for you. Happiness is not found through finding a soul mate, but through finding satisfaction in a loving Savior who has called you his own and made you a beloved son or daughter of the King.

2. <u>**Decide what you want your life to look like and start planting seeds for your future:**</u>

This is the time to prepare your dreams and plant intentional and purposeful seeds knowing that life in itself can change drastically at harvest time. There are some things you need to put in place in your life before you meet your intended spouse. What are those things you are waiting to do until you find a spouse? If you can do these things alone, then there is nothing stopping you. Start cultivating a savings habit, start developing yourself in every area, start fulfilling purpose and start making an impact in the lives of people. Then when the spouse comes, he or she will be able to support your vision and purpose. But you must start first. Get on it.

3. **Take Risks:**

Trust that no matter where you are if God's plan is for you to marry, He will lead you to just the right person, and at the right time. Is there something you have always wanted to try? Now is the time when you are by yourself and not bound by finances or sharing time with another. Go for it. Experiment with life now that you have the chance while you have no one else to subject to your experimentations. Do what you have never done but would love to do. Open yourself up to a world of possibilities and have the time of your life because this season will eventually pass. You can be the one to mobilise all your single friends for a gathering, a hangout, an event you think would be beneficial to their lives, etc. I loved this about myself. I didn't know how to keep information to myself when I come across an event that would be very beneficial and uplifting to me. I would start messaging and calling and even compelling friends to clear their schedule and find time to attend the event. It sure didn't take them long enough to identify me as the friend that brings everyone together. Asides the fact that I loved to see my friends, I just didn't want to keep the knowledge and wisdom to myself alone. I had to share it, even if that involved always calling people.

This time of freedom will not last forever. It will only last for a while. And as such, having a partner might change some things so that it will not be possible to be so carefree, fancy-free or footloose about things any longer.

WHAT TO DO WITH YOUR SINGLENESS

There are so many benefits of singleness and what you can do to embrace your season totally. One person rightly stated. "Don't do something about your singleness or singlehood but do something with it". There is a difference. Trying to do something about your singleness, leaves an impression that you are trying to get out of that season by all means and on the other hand, doing something with your singleness, connotes embracing the season, being content and serving purpose in that season. Let's discuss some of the things you can do in singleness.

1. <u>**Single but in a relationship with Christ.**</u>

This is where you trust God with your singleness and your season. This is the period to nurture, grow and deepen your relationship with Christ. Ideally, there is no one taking the first place in your life, but Christ so put Him first and keep Him there regardless of your relationship status.

Are you growing in maturity, are you growing in the qualities that matter most to you and God regardless of your relationship status, are you embracing your singleness? You will know you are embracing your singleness when you truly recognise who you are, and you do not need another person to relieve you of the feeling, and you are not overwhelmed with a false sense of inadequacy. Singleness gives you more room to be open with Christ. Your relationship with Christ should be bigger than any of your other relationships. In Singleness, knowing who you are in Christ will help a great deal in making decisions, and walking through life regardless of your relationship status.

If Christ remains first place in your life, when the singleness phase is over, and you have to give another person a position in your life, you will have no problem ensuring the person rightly takes the position of second place. That is how it ought to be. Cultivate your relationship with Him (Christ) first.

2. Deepen and strengthen your relationship with God

As a follow-up from the first point above, you can only deepen your relationship with God when you have an existing relationship with Him. To have a healthy long-lasting relationship with others, you first of all have to introduce yourselves to each other and always make an effort to grow your friendship or relationship for you to feel comfortable with each other. Likewise, deepening your relationship with God enables you to come to a place of knowledge, comfort and acceptance of who you are and who God says you are.

With the way God loves and cares for us, deepening our relationship with Him, makes us understand that with all our temperament and other things we do not like about ourselves, Gods love for us does not fluctuate. This, in turn, teaches us to show love to others the way Christ shows love to us. If you desire to deepen your relationship with God, practising honest communication with Him regularly would be a starting point. Learn to speak to him regularly; trusting Him because when he had no reason, he still loved you unconditionally. You should be able to open up and let God into every area, room and department of your life. This relationship with Christ should be continuous at every stage of your life, as that would guide you through other relationships with men and women.

When you have cultivated a deep relationship with God, you find that when people love you regardless of your background, regardless of your past, regardless of your relationship status, regardless of your flaws, you remember the love Christ has for you and you know that this is a Christ-like love. This is the love we must emulate, but this can only be achieved through a deeper relationship with God.

3. Life of Service

One advantage of being single as was mentioned above is so that we might 'serve the Lord best with as few distractions as possible' *1*

Corinthians 7:35. As much as marriage can be a beautiful thing, there is no doubt in my mind that a spouse can be a dear distraction as well. When you have a spouse, you wonder 'how do I please my spouse', 'how do I please and satisfy my children', etc. so you spend your days in this pursuit of worldly worries.

On the other hand, singleness can give you the freedom to volunteer in church, investigate short and long-term mission opportunities and you would only be in a pursuit of 'How to please your Lord' without the all-absorbing duties of a spouse and children. In other words, the advantage of the solitary life is that without the distraction of an earthly spouse, the need of the heavenly father can be met. Your single season is a great time to serve. No doubt unmarried men and women have been found to be focused on how to please God when there is no distraction; this is because we would usually have the time, attention and energy to give. Married people may often find that they have to juggle divided loyalties. This is the truth.

So what joy and unbounded freedom is yours if you are privileged to live a single life. Challenge yourself to live life every day continuously discovering the sweet surprises of the single life while you still have it.

Get committed to a service at a local church, volunteer at a Charity home, reach out to the voiceless, become a contributor and not a consumer and become a servant in the Kingdom of God. You would find that you begin to develop the strength of selflessness, accomplishments and satisfaction. Remember that active leadership in other areas of your life, will in some way prepare you for leadership and submission of a family in the future. Remember Paul's words to Timothy in *'1 Tim 4:12* – 'Let no one think less of you because you are young. Be an example to all believers in what you say, in the way you live, in your love, in your faith and your purity'. So, seek the Kingdom of God above all else and live righteously, and He will give you everything you need - *Matthew 6: 33*.

Also, read books on relationships and marriage, attend courtship seminars, find out and learn what love, dating, courting and marriage is all about. 'For I know the plans I have for you, says the Lord, they are plans for good and not for disaster, to give you a future and hope - *Jeremiah 29: 11*. If you have been called to marriage in your future, you should be passionate to want to find out what it entails.

4. <u>Single but with the Fruits of the Spirit.</u>

More importantly, the singleness phase is where you check yourself and daily grow in the fruits of the spirit. The fruits of the spirit are love, joy peace, patience, faithfulness, goodness, kindness, gentleness and self-control. In singleness, you should intentionally cultivate the habit of developing the fruits of the spirit in your daily living. You should love on purpose, be kind on purpose, be patient on purpose, be joyful on purpose, be good on purpose, be gentle on purpose, be faithful on purpose, exercise self-control on purpose and find peace with all men on purpose.

Regardless of your relationship status, the devil works diligently every day, looking for ways to steal our peace. We, therefore, should intentionally and purposely find peace with ourselves, peace with men and peace with God.

If you have been called to marriage, trust God to make it come to pass. Many at times, we choose to move faster than God and go ahead to seek what we earnestly desire. Now what happens is that God would sometimes allow us to remain in certain circumstances so that we can learn one or two things from experience. This is where faith and patience as fruits of the spirit come in. The wait in singleness tests our character to see if we are mature enough to get what we asked for from God. As Christians, the fruits of the spirit are very vital in growing in Christ and being content with whatever relationship status we find ourselves in. It is possible that God will not want to give you a partner if you do not know how to love, control yourself, be patient, be kind, be peaceful, be faithful, be good, be joyful or be gentle. You would need to intentionally develop yourself in the fruits of the spirit before getting into a relationship. This exercise would equally enable you to easily discern the fruits of the spirit in a possible future partner's life. Just as was said in the bible, 'By their fruits you shall know them'. A fruit can only hide its true self for long, but with perseverance and a good discerning spirit, its true self will be revealed.

5. Single but Complete

'My better half', 'we complete each other'. Do these phrases sound familiar? Very much I would say. In today's world, there are teachings that because God caused a deep sleep to befall Adam, and created Eve out of one of Adam's rib, a woman is now a part of the body of a man and once a man finds a woman to marry, he has then found his missing rib and as such she completes him. To be single does not in any way, shape or form mean you are half, needing another half to be complete.

Notice from our earlier discussion above, not everyone is called to marriage in *Matthew 19* and as such whether single or married, a single individual is a complete individual. There are no halves. Marriage can be as good as your single life. It would, therefore, be wrong to come into a marriage with the idea of completing another person. Therefore, in singleness we ought to live life to fulfil purpose as a whole and complete person. You do not need to be married to fulfil purpose. A single person serving God in singleness and a married person also serving God in marriage are complete individuals regardless of their relationship status.

We tend to think that because you are a certain type of way you would need a spouse to complete you in areas that you consider yourself deficient in. No. No one is deficient. Christ created us as singles, as individuals complete on our own. Imagine two 'incomplete' individuals coming together in marriage, trying daily to complete each other; this would be a difficult task. But when you come together as complete individuals, both will blend easily and can then work together to help each other fulfil purpose. Two complete individuals are stronger than two incomplete individuals.

Your identity and your wholeness should not come from any human being because your identity and wholeness can only be found in Christ. The moment you make that person you are dating or even your spouse the person that completes you or makes you whole, you will more or less end up idolising that person. *Romans 1:25* tells us that 'They traded the truth about God for a lie. So, they worshipped and served the things God created instead of the Creator himself, who is worthy of eternal praise! Amen'. This means that we should put our creator first and should not take pleasure in putting any other first. Never allow any other person to be your identity, let your identity be in Christ.

6. <u>Single but Happy.</u>

Happiness is a choice, an intentional choice. Happiness is a state of mind. Nobody can make you happy except yourself. A car, a house or a baby can only be new for so long, and our happiness starts to depreciate. What usually happens is that those things do not in any way bring us happiness, you decide for yourself to intentionally find and derive pleasure from the new house and car you just bought. You choose to find happiness in being part of the creation of a baby; you decide to find happiness in anything you want to regardless of your relationship status. Nobody can determine your happiness except yourself.

In singleness, be determined to be cheerful, happy and joyful in whatever situation you find yourself, for the greater part of our unhappiness at times is not determined by our circumstance but rather by our disposition to those circumstances. The truth is you can only be as happy as you make up your mind to be. Groucho Marx said 'I, not events, have the power to make me happy or unhappy today. I can choose which it shall be. Yesterday is dead; tomorrow hasn't arrived yet. I have just one day, today, and I'm, going to be happy in it'.

Happiness is a byproduct of enjoying the journey of life. However, in other to experience this happiness we are talking about, one must adopt the right and healthy attitude which allows you decide to be happy or not. In other words, I dare say your attitude in any given circumstance will determine your choice to be happy or not.

As commonly observed, when you ask people dating 'Why do you love him?' you would usually get the response 'Because he makes me happy'. No, you have decided to have a positive attitude towards your partner's gestures or advances which in turn makes you happy because you chose to be happy. No one can make you happy; you choose to find happiness in the comfort a friend shows you or you choose to find happiness in being able to achieve your goals because you went to the University.

There are days when you might not be happy. That's perfectly okay because circumstances in most cases determine our happiness. It should be known that the constant struggle to always be happy could lead to unhappiness in the long run. However, if you find that what you do gives you the happiness you desire, keep at it and do not expect anyone to make you happier.

Here are a few intentional ways to be happy and find contentment. Note that this list is not exhaustive as there are a million ways to be happy depending on what you choose.

1. **Count your blessings:** Ever so often we get caught in our worries and setbacks wondering why our lives had to take certain turns, try for once to count your blessings, I guarantee you, you would lose count. Choose to stay positive and grateful; this should provide the right and healthy mindset to stay happy.
2. **Try a smile:** No doubt, this lightens up a face that is down with worries. Even a fake smile sometimes makes you feel better because the strength you pulled together to make the smile on your face could also be comforting that everything would be alright regardless of your relationship status.
3. **Speak Affirmative words to yourself:** Affirmations are positive thoughts accompanied with affirmative beliefs and personal statements of truth. Daily intentional affirmations can

gradually heal a broken heart, put a smile on your face, build up your confidence, make you stronger and make you more effective regardless of your relationship status.

4. **Do something fun:** There is happiness and fulfillment in doing what you love doing. I love exercising it's always so refreshing when I work out either at the gym, at home, in a park, either alone or in a group. To know that you have intentionally devoted time and energy to exercise, games, movies, camping, hiking, kayaking, travelling, etc. is one of the most satisfying feelings you'll ever experience. You find that this enables you to intentionally grow in self-discipline and personal improvement.

5. **Explore your talents:** We all have gifts and talents which when explored leave us with a sense of fulfillment and happiness. Choose to work with your gifts and talents each day, for yourself and others, regardless of your relationship status; this would bring you unending joy.

6. **Treat others well:** This cannot be over-emphasized as this importantly transcends to life outside singleness. The Golden Rule states: Treat everyone you meet with kindness, patience and grace. This does not only benefit the receiver but also leaves a sense of growing satisfaction in the giver. The Bible also reminds us to treat others the way we want to be treated. If this becomes an intentional habit, you find that this would not be a problem for you during the dating phase.

7. **Search for joy in your pain:** Life is not meant to be easy, so also is life not supposed to be that difficult, but we acknowledge that we all encounter pain at some point. Pain if compared to what we all encounter is just subjective. When challenges are encountered, remind yourself that trials of life may be difficult, they don't, however, last forever, it will surely pass. As difficult as this may sound, try to find meaning in your pain, try to find a reason not to give up but to hold on. When you do this, perseverance and strength are being built and no doubt this goes a long way outside singleness in a long-lasting relationship.

REFLECTIONS

CHAPTER FOUR

DEFECTIVE DATING AND SITUATIONSHIPS

"If it's not a friendship or a relationship, it is a situationship; know the difference".

— Tolu Fabiyi

Yes! If you did not know, now you know, there are such things as situation-ships and defective dating. These days, people do not value or appreciate a solid companionship the right way. The idea of a being in a relationship has now become so diluted and uncommon because people are more individualistic and anything that takes time and patience is regarded as a burden. We want things here and right now.

By way of definition, defective dating is like wanting to pay a driving instructor to learn to drive an Aston Martin Race Car, but along the way, you changed your mind and decided to pay someone else to learn how to ride a bicycle. In other words, it is fair to say defective dating is swerving off course from the highway into the busy roads when driving. There are usually more options to turn left, right, go straight or take a corner which then gives birth to situation-ships. In other words, defective dating leads to situation-ships.

A situation-ship is a pseudo-relationship - A placebo masking itself as a formative relationship. It looks and smells like a relationship, and it may even feel like one, but in most cases, it is not. Dictionary describes a situation-ship as any problematic relationship characterised by one or more unresolved, interpersonal conflicts. Situation-ships are usually confused with dating or being in a relationship.

The overall dating climate today is changing rapidly, and formalities are harder to find. Some seem to think those formalities have been eradicated. Instead, there is this awkward journeying through something that feels like something that leads to sex that may or may not be something that continues for a time until one party wants to make it an something official. It sure feels like a relationship, and to everyone else, it may seem like one, but to you and your partner, it sure isn't.

We have moved from the intentional way of dating and replaced it with the modern style of situation-ship. Have you ever asked someone, or have you ever been asked if you are dating a certain Mr. D? If you get a response, or your initial reply comes out in the form of mumbles, a little laughter and then the words like 'no not really' or 'yeah, we have an understanding' or 'no, we are just seeing each other' or 'we are not there yet' etc. Then, my dear, it is either you are just friends, or it is likely that that relationship has started showing signs of being defective and then becoming a situation-ship. Take for instance, you attend a family function and your old aunt asks, "you have a boyfriend or girlfriend yet darling?" Then you stutter and say oh no aunt, I'm still very single. Are you though? Or are you simply afraid of your truth, because the truth will be that you are in some type of relationship, you are just not sure what exactly it is just yet. And until you are, you might as well keep it that way.

Let's face it. A lot of people engage in situation-ships like it is the newest tourist location. It's almost like there is some comfort in being in a situation-ship compared to being on the single platform, waiting on the dating train to pull up. To date with purpose is the complete reverse of situation-ships.

LET'S LOOK AT SEVEN SIGNS YOU ARE IN A SITUATION-SHIP.

1. You don't have a title

Although the title 'boyfriend', 'girlfriend', 'in a relationship' etc. does not solely define a union, a title is an important indication in any relationship situation you find yourself. Take for instance; Luke is without employment, and his friend Janet draws his attention to a Butterfield company indicating that they have some vacancies available and Luke could apply to one of them. Luke instead sends an email to the HR and recruiting department indicating his skills and interest for any job at the organisation. The recruitment team sees his CV and decides to hire him as he has the skills they need in the organisation. Upon hiring, Luke finds that every working day he does different activities and moves around all the ten departments in the organisation. He complains to the HR department and to his amazement, he was informed that he did not apply for a specific job title at the organisation and as such he cannot be assigned a specific set of roles. So, his job had no title, he just kept working for the company. Likewise, when you don't know what to call him or her when confronted with situations of introduction or mere mention, then you know you don't have a title to your situation. Because you are not sure what to call him or her, you find that you frequently find yourself fumbling to find words to describe your situation-ship 'I mean we're not really….we really care for each other, so we're taking it slow you know'. If the situation is not interrupted by communication and asking specific questions, both will remain in the situation-ship for as long as they can, remaining title less.

2. You still attend events solo

In most cases, because you are not sure of your status with him or her, you avoid having to exercise your right to a plus one at weddings, Christmas parties, birthdays and family occasions. You would rather spare yourself mind boggling conversations. You try to convince yourself "you don't want to push things and you are not there yet" even though from the look of things, you are there in every other way. You may need to re-evaluate your thoughts as you are practising being in a situation-ship.

3. You haven't met their friends or family and they haven't met yours yet

By now, you know too well that this must be some kind of situation if your close friends know you are seeing someone and have been for a while, but they have never met this person. If you both practice the things being practised in the dating world today or you have been 'seeing each other' for a reasonable length of time and you still feel the need to keep him or her behind closed doors – this may be an indication of uncertainty. You know you are not sure and it's safer if only you, know how unsure you are. This could be a situation-ship.

4. You feed intimacy without commitment

Did you know that a good percentage of people in 'relationships', practice intimacy as a major way of showing love to their partners? Deepening intimacy on any level without defining a sense of commitment to each other is plainly dangerous. It's like going mountain climbing with a partner who is not sure they want to be tasked with the responsibility of holding your rope. You might think both cases are different. Think about it carefully. When you have succeeded in climbing one thousand feet, you wouldn't want your partner to tell you how tired they feel going further up together. Likewise, in a relationship, intimacy without commitment is plainly dangerous as it only prepares the room for the conversation of rejection and abandonment when one party suddenly feels tired physically and emotionally to continue the journey. The Bible *in 1 Thessalonians 4:6* refers to this as defrauding, ripping someone off by raising expectations but not delivering on the promise. Joshua Harris puts it this way "Intimacy without commitment is like icing without a cake, it can be sweet, but it ends up us making us sick".

5. You are discontent with God's gift of singleness

Ladies, do you have friends that are just never single? They are always in one relationship or the other and there's never really room to breathe. Defective dating and situation-ships cause dissatisfaction because it instills some form of discontentment in our minds. We become accustomed to wanting companionship, to expressing love by being intimate and to idolizing a fellow individual because we believe they are the source of our happiness. A string of uncommitted dating relationships is simply situation-ships. It causes people to focus on what they don't have as the yardstick for living as opposed to enjoying the unique qualities of singleness while you have it.

6. You are distracted from fulfilling purpose and other vital relationships

This is where defective dating encourages us to compromise on our values and standards. When all you do is spend time with him or her and talk about him or her, you find that you would begin to shift your plans and schedules and would give anything to be with him or her, even if this meant giving up weekly bible study sessions, gym sessions or other personal development opportunities. By its common definition, dating involves two people focusing on each other. Unfortunately, and in most cases, the rest of the world fades into the background because the world is now about the both of you only. When you isolate yourself from other vital relationships and fulfilling purpose as you should, you put yourself in a precarious situation – situation-ship.

7. When you both decide to have an open relationship.

While I was growing up in secondary school, I liked a friend of mine who had an interest in someone else at the time. Time passed, I never told him about it, but we kept up as good friends even after school. We both moved to different countries, kept in touch and even grew closer and stronger as friends. Finally, after about a year, I came out to him on how I felt back in school, and as you would imagine, he claimed to have known about it but just didn't want to say anything. Thankfully, this didn't bother our friendship, but it sure took a turn into a 'situation-ship' as we were in different countries and could not afford to start an across the ocean relationship. It was never a situation where he asked me out and I responded with blushes and a loud yes with me grinning from side to side. It was more like, we really enjoyed each other's company and somehow things just kicked off and we found ourselves wanting to be in a relationship, but our circumstance left us considering having an open relationship - 'situation-ship'. So, we were not in a relationship but in our minds, it felt like we were.

As you would imagine neither of really asked questions or wanted to define whatever it was we were doing. Mind you; we were both 18 years of age at the time so one would not have expected much of us especially as we did not exactly understand the whole love and dating thing. We just really liked each other and wanted it to remain that way. I had no idea what an open relationship was or was not, but because I was keen on holding on to what we had, I was very much open to the idea. We tried it for a while, but it did not make much sense and we could not hold on for long. This was clearly one kind of a situation-ship we found ourselves in. Along the line, we re-adjusted our thoughts on love and dating and decided to keep it as friends.

An open relationship is a defective relationship. It's not a relationship but a situation-ship and without proper understanding, this experience will have you investing time, energy, emotions and other resources in what you have no control over.

WHAT TO DO TO AVOID DEFECTIVE DATING AND SITUATION-SHIPS.

1. Be Honest

Be honest with yourself. Only you in your situation know exactly how you feel. Denying the absence of purpose amid situation-ships is a pointer as to what is missing in your 'relationship'. There should be nothing to hide. We all agree that love and dating is a journey, so why risk going through the entire trip only to have bad memories about it, when you could have tried the honesty card along the way to make better memories. If you think you are in what seems like a 'situation-ship', you can start by being honest. Accept your situation for what it is and seek intentional ways to purposeful dating.

2. Communicate and Ask Questions

Knowledge is power. To get knowledge, you must seek, communicate and ask questions intentionally. In every relationship, when questions are not asked, we tend to make assumptions which in turn lead to failed expectations. But the catch here is we tend to repeat the same cycle repeatedly. Try communicating and asking the questions mentioned in chapter seven of this book, in a manner that would yield well thought out and honest conversations.

3. Pay Attention

There is no point asking questions and communicating if you have no intention of paying attention to the answers you receive. Ask questions not just because you want the questions to be asked but because you desire to get answers. Pay close attention to what people say, watch out for the triggers and warning signs. Remember, the devil is in the detail. Most times, we ask questions and skillfully sift through the response we get in other to find and choose what response we want to hear and accept. This time around, don't sift through the replies or answers; take everything on board, pay attention to what is said and what is not said.

For instance, if you ask me if I am hungry and I reply saying 'not really', somewhere in my response could indicate to you that 'I am not hungry at the moment but will be later'. I believe with time; people tend to show you who they truly are, including those who have mastered the art of long life pretence. So, ask yourself, what are you paying attention to – intimacy, gifts, choice of words, actions, etc. and how do they define your 'relationship'.

REFLECTIONS

CHAPTER FIVE

INTRODUCING LOVE

__Don't excite love, don't stir it up, until the time is ripe,__
__and you are ready"__

— Songs of Solomon 8:4 (The Message)

Selfless love is Supreme. Selfless love is the priority of every Christian and should be of every human on earth. Love is not an emotion but a way of life. Love is a word that can only be adequately defined in terms of action, attitude, words and behaviour. Paul in the bible explains fifteen (15) characteristics of love to show us what love in everyday life should look like.

One of the words used to describe LOVE as we know it is AGAPE (Agape Love). Sometimes this notion of Agape love comes across to us as if we are unfriendly, when in fact Agape isn't really friendliness, it is self-denial for the sake of another. It is a love that loves without changing. It is a self-giving love that gives without demanding or expecting repayment. It is love so great that it can be given to the unlovable or unappealing. It is love that loves even when it is rejected. Agape love gives and loves because it wants to; it does not demand or expect repayment from the love given. It gives because it loves, it does not love in order to receive.

A whole series of teachings could easily be taught on these qualities and attributes of love. But let's look briefly at each of them. For the sake of better explanation, we would divide this into two parts: what love is; and what love is not.

WHAT LOVE IS NOT:

1. Love is not jealous: Jealously and envy accomplishes nothing but rather destroys the growth of the one who envies. Jealousy relates to greed and selfishness. The jealous person wants what others have; he wants things for himself. He is too selfish to applaud others' success; he has to have all the attention. You would usually find that jealously implies one is displeased with the success of another. On the contrary, true love desires the success of others. Love keeps its distance from envy and does not resent it when someone else succeeds. Remember love is selfless. Try praying for someone you envy, pray for more success for them and you would find your mind at peace because love and envy cannot reside together. If you avoid jealousy or envy, you would be able to show love to others regardless of your relationship status or your present season in life.

   ❖ Apply this to your everyday life. What does this mean to you?

   _____

   _____

   _____

2. Love does not brag: Bragging in its actual sense is trying to make someone feel jealous of what we have or trying to stir discontentment in the lives of others. When you and I brag, we are demonstrating our insecurity and spiritual immaturity. Love in action can work anonymously. It does not have to have the limelight or the attention to do a good job, or to be satisfied with the result. Love gives because it loves to give, not out of the sense of praise it can have from showing itself off.

Sometimes (not always the case) the people who work the hardest at love are those the furthest from it. They do things many would perceive as loving, yet they do them in a manner which would parade itself. This does not sound like love; it is pride looking for glory by the appearance of love. Paul states that bragging is the reverse of biblical love. Hence, we should pursue Christ so that we will be humble before Him and others.

❖ Apply this to your daily life. What does this mean to you?

_____

_____

_____

3. <u>Love is not arrogant:</u> Arrogance refers to a raving desire for power. To be arrogant is only rooted in pride. William Carey is thought by many to be the founder of the modern missionary movement. Christians all over the world knew who he was and honored him. He came from a humble place; he was a shoe repairman when God called him to reach the world. Once, when Carey was at a dinner party, a snobbish Lord tried to insult him by saying very loudly, "Mr. Carey, I hear you once were a shoemaker!" Carey replied, "No, your Lordship, not a shoemaker, only a cobbler!" Today, the name of William Carey is remembered, but nobody remembers who that snobbish Lord was! His love showed itself in not having a big head about himself.

Arrogance disrespects others and carries a disdain for others. God calls us to serve others and be gracious toward them. Leave no room for pride.

❖ Apply this to your daily life. What does this mean to you?

_____

_____

_____

4. <u>Love does not act unbecomingly</u>: Love is not rude, for where there is love; there will be kindness and good manners. It is courteous, polite and sensitive to the feelings of others. The reason we are not courteous, of course, is that we are thinking only of ourselves and not of others. In other words, for love not to be rude, love has to be selfless.

Some Christians believe in saying it as it is, however, but love doesn't always tell it like it is; it doesn't always verbalise all its thoughts, particularly if those thoughts don't build others up. Let your words and actions of love be to build others up in your relationships, at home, at work and in every season of your life.

❖ Apply this to your daily life. What does this mean to you?

_____

_____

_____

5. <u>Love is not provoked</u>: Notice that Paul did not say 'love is not <u>easily</u> provoked'. So, the requirement is not whether you are easily provoked or not but whether you are provoked at all. We all find it easy to be provoked, to become irritated with those who are just plain annoying. But practice being intentional about showing love and make sure your love is not provoked.

❖ Apply this to your daily life. What does this mean to you?

_____

_____

_____

6. <u>Love does not take into account record of wrongs suffered</u>: Literally, this means "love does not store up the memory of any wrong it has received." Love will put away the hurts of the past instead of clinging to them. Love offers Grace. This means not being cruel or judgmental with the truth. You have to embrace

the Grace of God before you can freely share it with others. *Colossians 3:13-14* – Make allowance for each other's fault and forgive anyone who offends you. Remember the Lord forgave you, so you must forgive others. Above all, clothe yourselves with love, which binds us all together in perfect harmony.

One married man said to his friend, "You know, every time my wife and I get into a conflict, she gets historical." His friend said, "Historical? Don't you mean hysterical?" "No, I mean historical. She rehearses everything I've ever done wrong in the whole history of our marriage." That's keeping score! That's not love.

Love doesn't keep a tally of wrongs and bear a grudge until every one of the wrong is paid for. It doesn't try to gain the upper hand by reminding the other person of past wrongs. Love forgives.

❖ Apply this to your daily life. What does this mean to you?

_____

_____

_____

7. <u>Love does not rejoice in unrighteousness:</u> Love takes no joy in evil of any kind. It takes no malicious pleasure when it hears about the inadequacies, mistakes, and sins of someone else. Love is righteous.

There is a delicate balance to love. Although love is kind and overlooks the faults of others, it does not compromise the truth or take a soft view of sin. To allow another person to go on in sin, whether it is known sin, or a blind spot is not to seek his best; it is not love. Love will sensitively confront and correct precisely because it cares deeply and knows that sin destroys.

❖ Apply this to your daily life. What does this mean to you?

_____

_____

_____

WHAT LOVE IS:

1. <u>Love is patient:</u> Patience is an interesting quality. Paul seems to be saying that love does not have a short fuse. It does not lose its temper quickly. A person who exercises agape love does not lose patience with people. Love never says, "I'll give you just one more chance." Love is patient. The Greek word comes from two words meaning, "long-tempered." If you are patient it means you should be slow to anger; you endure personal wrongs without retaliating, you bear with others' imperfections, faults, and differences. You give them time to change, room to make mistakes without coming down hard on them.

   If God's love is in us, we will be longsuffering to those who offend, annoy, irritate and hurt us.

   ❖ Apply this to your daily life. What does this mean to you?

   _____

   _____

   _____

2. <u>Love is kind:</u> This has to do with the way we speak. The same sentence can have two different meanings, depending on how you say it. Sometimes our words could mean one thing while we said it, but because of the tone in our voice, our words to another person could mean something entirely different. In other words, we end up sending double messages which later open doors for resentments, lack of communication and misunderstanding amongst people. Although you may not be responsible for how someone chooses to understand words when spoken, what you can be responsible for is how you say those words.

   Kindness can also be likened to patience in action. When we have and show God's love, it will be seen in simple acts of kindness. Kindness means to withhold what harms, as well as give what heals. Love is kind, but often tough.

The kind person shows kindness in response to harsh treatment. Jesus said, "And if you do good to those who do good to you, what credit is that to you? For even sinners do the same thing. . . But love your enemies, and do good, and lend, expecting nothing in return; and your reward will be great, and you will be sons of the Most High; for He, Himself is kind to ungrateful and evil men" *(Luke 6:33, 35)*. Our kindness motivates others toward positive change of attitude.

❖ Apply this to your daily life. What does this mean to you?

_____

_____

_____

3. <u>Love rejoices in the truth:</u> Love rejoices with the truth. Love gets excited when it hears of spiritual victories. Love encourages by expressing joy over little evidence of growth. John, the apostle of love, wrote, "I have no greater joy than this, to hear of my children walking in the truth" *(3 John 4)*.

Love speaks the truth. *Ephesians 4:15* – Instead, we will tell the truth in love, growing in every way more and more like Christ, who is the head of his body, the church. And it goes further to say in *John 8:32* that 'you will know the truth and the truth will set you free'.

❖ Apply this to your daily life. What does this mean to you?

_____

_____

_____

4. <u>Love bears all things</u>: The word bears can also be translated to mean covers. To protect by covering. Love defends the character of the other person as much as possible within the limits of truth. Love will not lie about weaknesses, but neither will it deliberately expose and emphasize them. Love protects. One thing I was always conscious of doing while I was dating was never to expose the weakness of my partner to people outside deliberately. Instead, I would not say anything if I was not comfortable saying it. Do you intentionally expose your partner or friend in public or do you protect their weaknesses?

Love stands in the presence of a fault, with a finger on her lip." (Spurgeon)

❖ Apply this to your daily life. What does this mean to you?

   _____
   _____
   _____

5. <u>Love believes all things:</u> This is not to say that love is gullible. It does, however, mean that love is not suspicious and doubting of the other person's character and motives without good reason, even if his actions offended you. If trust has been broken, then it needs to be earned again, step by step. But love believes the other person is innocent until proven guilty. If there is a problem, love doesn't jump immediately to blame the other person.

Love is always ready to allow for extenuating circumstances, to give the other person the benefit of the doubt, to believe the best about people. If you treat yourself as if you were the most beautiful person in the world, you will be transformed before your very eyes. That's what Jesus did. To vacillating Simon, He said, "You are a rock." To a prostitute, He said, "Your sins are forgiven." To a woman caught in adultery, He said, "Neither do I condemn you. Go and sin no more." It is the simple power of believing the best and not the worst about yourself and other people.

❖ Apply this to your daily life. What does this mean to you?

_____

_____

_____

6. <u>Love hopes all things</u>: This is simply a step beyond believing. Here, Paul is teaching the power of positive thinking. But he is suggesting that love refuses to take failure as final, either in oneself or someone else. Love never gives up on people. And the reason the believer can take such an attitude is that God is in the business of taking human failures and producing spiritual giants out of them.

Love has confidence in the future and not pessimism. When hurt, it does not say, "It will be this way forever and even get worse." It hopes for the best, and it hopes in God. Love rests on the promises of God that He is working all things together for good for those who love Him and are called according to His purpose.

❖ Apply this to your daily life. What does this mean to you?

_____

_____

_____

7. <u>Love endures all things</u>: The greatness of agape love is it keeps on bearing, believing, and hoping. It doesn't give up. Love holds fast to people it loves. It perseveres. It never gives up on anyone. Love won't stop loving, even in the face of rejection. Love takes action to shake up an intolerable situation. Love looks beyond the present to the hope of what might be in the future.

❖ Apply this to your daily life. What does this mean to you?

_____

_____

_____

8. <u>Love never fails:</u> This is the permanence and supremacy of love. When Paul says love never fails, he means love never ends. Love lives forever.

Some days seem like victory, and other days we feel defeated. It's easy to look around and be discouraged on the hard days because we forget that the end of the story is already written and at the end 'we win'.

Love never fails. But whether there are prophecies, they will fail; whether there are tongues, they will cease; whether there is knowledge, it will vanish away.

You have to embrace the love of Christ in your life before modelling such example in your singleness, your relationship or whatever season you find yourself. 1 Corinthians 13:13 – Three things will last forever – faith, hope and love – and the greatest of these is love.

❖ Apply this to your daily life. What does this mean to you?

_____

_____

_____

No one is expected to joyfully tick off all the fifteen expressions of love with a score of 100% just like that. Love is a journey. Love is your journey. So, it is not a race ran at your own pace, practice showing love to your friends, family and partner in different ways till it becomes a daily routine and a part of your journey. Remember it is a lifestyle and experiencing the love of Christ is vital to us showing love to others. When we seek and understand an intra-personal relationship (relationship with yourself) as well as a relationship with God, we are likely to succeed at an interpersonal relationship (relationship with others).

Ask yourself, today, how will you grow in your love for yourself and for others? First, I would suggest that you cannot become the loving person you desire to be without a loving and vibrant relationship with God. This love relationship must be cultivated first and foremost. In whatever circumstance you find yourself, work through Paul's letter on love and find where you stand. Daily develop a habit of loving members of your family, your coworkers, and strangers on the streets, your neighbours and even your enemies. Once you can do this, you will be able to better love the world around you. Remember that without love as the motive and goal, the gifts are meaningless distractions. Losing love breaks relationships. God has called us to love people regardless of our relationship status. Jesus said that all people would know we are His disciples by the love that we have for one another *(John 13:34-35)*. He has called us to love with every season of our lives on earth.

Singleness is not a sin. As long as you remain alive and you continue to walk intentionally in purpose there is hope, and you are a day closer to your next season according to God's timetable for you. It is okay to be single; you are not 'less' because you are single, you are not forgotten neither are you incomplete. When you have your eyesight too far into the future, sometimes, you lose sight of what you ought to do today. All you have to do is to be content where you are and maximise the season you find yourself regardless of your relationship status. Never think of yourself as inferior to others because you are in a different season of your life. Remember at the right time; you will get to your next season when you need to get there. Your lane is your process and your personal journey, so be intentional about focusing and enjoying your journey. Maximise your seasons and grow in love within you and around you.

REFLECTIONS

CHAPTER SIX

PURPOSE OF DATING

"The mystery of human existence lies not in just staying alive, but in finding something to live for."
— Fyodor Dostoyevsky, The Brothers Karamazov

"You were put on this earth to achieve your greatest self, to live out your purpose, and to do it courageously."
— Steve Maraboli, Life, the Truth, and Being Free

What exactly is the purpose of dating? What is the point of dating? Why do we even bother to date? Dou you date to find if you can go a long way with the opposite sex and in turn hopefully spend forever together? If this is why you date, then I would assume you are dating with a trajectory towards marriage. This means for you; dating has to be intentional. While the idea of dating with a path towards marriage is the goal in purposeful dating, it is also worth noting that the primary point of dating is to get to truly know people in other to willfully decide if you want to start a relationship with them! Simple isn't it. This again presupposes that dating has to be intentional from the beginning.

Dating with purpose is intentional, precise and directed; dating without purpose is stressful, purposeless, visionless and painful. No doubt, the search for relevance in life is one ultimate pursuit of a man on earth. Your purpose in life in everything far outweighs your wildest imagination or anything you know. The fact is, we were birthed by God through our parents to come into the world for a reason, for a purpose. To know and understand this purpose, we must begin with God.

WHAT IS PURPOSE?

Everything in life surely has a purpose, so also is everyone born with a purpose and for a purpose. Where such purpose is not known abuse becomes inevitable. Thus, if you are not aware of the purpose for which you date, you will abuse your singleness and make an abnormal use of dating. Your purpose is, therefore, an integral part of you and not of someone else. Discovering and understanding that purpose will no doubt impact your idea of purposeful dating.

You cannot make the mistake of living someone else's purpose and living your purpose through someone else's life. You are the way you are because of why you are. Never try to become like someone else. You are designed for your purpose, and you are perfect for your purpose. To remove your purpose would be to significantly change who you are because your purpose both informs and reveals your nature and your responsibilities. Everything you naturally have and inherently are is necessary for you to fulfil your purpose, not someone else's. Your height, your race, your skin colour, language, physical features and intellectual capacity are all designed for your purpose. Our individual purpose is linked to a greater purpose and as such the world needs you and the purpose for which you were born. Purpose keeps you focused.

Purpose is Gods will;
Purpose is life;
Purpose is the beginning and the end;

Purpose is the original reason for the existence of a thing;
Purpose is the destination that prompts the journey;
Purpose is the key to fulfilment.

Purpose cannot be overemphasised. Knowing that we were put on earth for a purpose, the never-ending questions of 'why' will always have to be answered. It is the 'why' that explains the reason for our actions and existence. Have you tried asking yourself why you do certain things, why you embark on individual missions, why you say certain things, why you live the way you do, why you go to church, why you do what you do and so on? Ask yourself these questions.

You will find that most times, one 'why' will lead to ten other 'whys' this is because you are not convinced as to the reasons you created for your actions. With this, you would have to keep asking yourself 'why' till your final goal gives you peace and conviction. This process is what I call finding purpose. It does not necessarily happen in a day, but it's a committed process of finding the truth behind what we do. This could take days, weeks, months, years or even a lifetime. But there is no greater joy on earth knowing that you found your purpose and fulfilled it.

This book is not about Purpose in its holistic view; rather it is about dating with a purpose and building intentional relationships. It is important to date with a purpose because your choices determine your life. *Proverbs 18:22* says 'He that finds a wife, finds a good thing and obtains favour from the Lord'. This reveals to us that there has to be a process of finding which presupposes an intentional search. You only find what you are seeking or searching for intentionally. However, to understand how to date with a purpose, you must understand what purpose is and how it plays a vital role in our daily lives which in turn affects everything we do (in singleness, dating and marriage). Just as the famous proverb says, 'where purpose is unknown, abuse will become inevitable'. In effect, if you do not know the purpose of dating you will abuse the idea of dating, and there will be no fulfillment. So, I dare say without purpose, there will be no fulfillment.

Here is a guide to understanding purpose as we walk through singleness into dating with purpose and into marriage for the rest of our lives.

Guide One: God is a God of Purpose: In the beginning, God had a plan. He never did anything without purpose. The creation of the Heavens, the Earth and you as an individual, was intentional and with purpose.

Guide Two: Everything in life has a purpose: Knowing that God is a God of purpose and He has created EVERYTHING with and for a purpose. Everything, down to the little creatures we detest or to the humans we also detest, they all serve a specific purpose. Just because we do not understand someone's purpose, does not mean that person is purposeless. In effect, ignorance of purpose does not negate or cancel the existence of purpose.

Guide Three: Where purpose is not known, abuse is inevitable: Have you done things in life and later on you tell yourself "I'm not sure why I did that"? As important as it is to always know the reason for what we do, sometimes purpose is unknown. This reminds us of the significant story of Jonah which explains what could happen when purpose is unknown. When God told Jonah to go to Nineveh, he refused and disobeyed. He tried to run away from God by boarding a ship that was sailing in the opposite direction. On route, a violent storm nearly broke the ship apart. The sailors were terrified and even threw some of their cargo into the sea in other to lessen the danger. During all this, Jonah was sleeping in the cabin of the ship.

Much later when the storm continued, the sailors decided to cast lots to see who was to blame for the danger and the lot fell on Jonah. Jonah then answered them saying 'I am a Hebrew and I worship the Lord, the God of Heaven, who made the sea and the land'. He further went ahead to tell the sailors of how God had sent him somewhere, and he was running away. He then asked that he be thrown into the sea in other for the storm to be calm. Finally, the sailors did, and the sea became calm.

Now the sailor's problem was not really the storm but not knowing the purpose of the storm. If the sailors had known Gods purpose for the storm, they would not have tried so hard to save themselves, as God was only trying to speak to Jonah. The fact that they lacked knowledge about the purpose of the storm did not negate the purpose of the storm. God's message to Jonah was still passed across. In effect, unknown purpose always wastes time and gives the possibility of danger.

Abuse of purpose then occurs whenever we don't use the created thing according to its creator's intention. If you do not know the purpose for a child, you will abuse and misuse the child (child abuse); If you do not know the purpose of education, you will misuse the opportunity to be educated; If you do not know the purpose of money, you will misuse the money, If you do not know the purpose of a job, you will abuse the job. Likewise, if you do not know the purpose of singleness, you will misuse your single stage, and If you do not know the purpose of dating, you will definitely abuse the relationship.

It is therefore essential that you either discover the purpose for everything you do or simply refrain from doing till you gain the knowledge of that purpose. Take for instance a friend asks to date you and this friend has no understanding of dating and equally does not understand its purpose. Be rest assured that until he discovers that God given purpose and gains that understanding, he will abuse you and that relationship unless of course, both parties seek to find that understanding along the journey.

Guide Four: Purpose is the key to fulfillment: Purpose dictates performance which in turn influences satisfaction. When a manufacturer produces a car he has an expectation, likewise when an individual purchases a car, he or she also has an expectation. Now if both expectations do not coincide, there will be no satisfaction nor fulfillment with the car. Imagine a car without a purpose; there would be no satisfaction for the consumer to enjoy and as such the car would be abused till it becomes worthless. In effect, you will never actually experience real fulfillment until you are working out the purpose for which you were created. Just like a trumpets purpose is fulfilled when it is blown, a guitar when it is skillfully strung, a car when it is safely driven, a seed when properly planted and becomes a tree, food consumed when hungry etc., so also is your fulfillment dependent on you discovering and fulfilling your purpose in every given circumstance.

Imagine a life of purpose; you live intentionally, you find purpose in everything you do, you find that whether the result is success or failure, there is fulfillment in the sense that you knew what you were going for and went for it intentionally. In all things, purpose is the key to fulfillment because it establishes the foundation on which all life must be built.

WHAT IS THE PURPOSE OF DATING?

1. We date because we want to get married: Dating can help couples acquire the needed knowledge and skills for a successful marriage. For example, dating helps develop a better understanding of each other's attitudes and behaviours, how to get along, and can increase your ability to discuss and solve relational problems. Dating provides you with the opportunity to refine your power of observation. It enables you to make certain what type of personality and disposition is best suited for you. Dating is the best opportunity for you to find your ideal spouse and to decide whether the person is the one you would want to spend your life with.

2. We date to get to know someone better: Dating is a process of discovery, getting to know yourself as much as it is getting to know the other. It's wise to go slow, so you can see how your partner handles a variety of situations in different circumstances before you make a lifetime commitment.

3. We date to get to know if both parties can be compatible.

4. We date to get to know if you can share and spend the rest of your life with someone else.

5. We date for social interaction: Wholesome dating experiences can prepare you for a happy, mature, and long-lasting marriage. Unwholesome dating, on the other hand, is fraught with the tragedy of a frail and shortened married life. We see this happen far too often.

6. We date because we need company.

7. We date because we need intimacy.

8. We date because we are scared of being alone.

9. We date because we love.

10. We date because we are tired of being single.

11. Dating helps you find the right mate: A person can use dating as a process of filtering out or narrowing the field of eligible partners down to a specific few and eventually to one person who will be his or her mate for a lifetime.

Ask yourself, why do you date?

REFLECTIONS

CHAPTER SEVEN

105 QUESTIONS TO BE ASKED WHEN DATING WITH PURPOSE

"Dating with no intent to marry is like going to the grocery shop without money, you either leave unhappy or take something that isn't yours":

— Jefferson Bethke

There are things we know we know; there are things we know we don't know, there are things we don't know we know and there are things we don't know that we don't know. The simple solution to these things we don't know is to communicate and ask questions. Sounds simple enough but it is also one of the major reasons for conflict amongst people.

This chapter emphasises the importance of being intentional and communicating effectively, by asking relevant questions before and during dating in other to ascertain whether you are making the right choice or not. Dating or Courtship is a time to gather information about your relevant other, assess and evaluate him or her and then come up with your conclusion, which would be your decision. *Amos 3:3* says 'can two walk together except they agree'? *Matthew 7:16* also says 'By their fruits, you shall know them'. Information is a weapon and knowledge is power.

Going through life can be likened to going on a field trip. We have left the safety of classroom (growing up in our families), and we will only arrive at our destination when Jesus comes. So, everything during the field trip is the journey. Remember being in junior school and going on a field trip? To keep you from wandering away or getting lost, the teacher paired you up with a friend and instructed you to hold hands and follow the group. Likewise, God has pretty much done the same thing for us. God has placed us in two different groups. One is the church which would prevent us from getting lost and help us to find our way to Christ. The second one is our spouse who will walk with you hand in hand towards Christ.

It is important to note that marriage is not the destination. We should be reminded that the world is only but a road to our destination and we are only passersby. The goal is attending the ultimate wedding to our Lord. This is the mindset needed for people who seek to date so that they would consciously date with the purpose of finding someone who they can walk hand in hand with and not let go of during their journey of life and ultimately present you before Christ at your final destination. This should guide your dating choices, if not you may need to press the pause button on dating, re-strategize on your purpose of dating and ask relevant intentional questions.

There must be a careful, intentional, deliberate and purposeful search for the truth. Your decision must be tested. It must be subjected to examination and analysis, in other to be able to determine its quality, its strength, its genuineness and alignment with God's word and purpose for your life.

Being single is the opportunity to become the kind you want to attract in life. Therefore, there are questions you ought to ask yourself and questions you ought to ask any person you seek to date. These questions must be intentional questions.

QUESTIONS

GOD'S ROLE IN YOUR MARRIAGE AND HOME

1. Is he or she a born again and a committed Christian?
2. Who is God to you?
3. What does salvation mean to you?
4. How important is spirituality to you?
5. Does he or she go to church?
6. What church does he or she go to?
7. Will we worship in the same church?
8. Will you be involved in service in church?
9. What is your understanding of the bible?
10. How much do I/he or she love God?
11. What is your view on sin?
12. Are we of the same faith, beliefs and values?
13. Will our relationship draw us closer to God?
14. Do we have peace in this relationship?
15. Can he or she meet my needs spiritually, physically, mentally and financially?
16. Can he or she encourage me to accomplish my purpose?
17. Can this person trust God to lead the way?
18. What is he or she's attitude towards forgiveness and repentance?
19. What is he or she's attitude towards co-habitation?
20. What is he or she's attitude towards purity?
21. What things would you do to ensure physical and spiritual purity?
22. Could you guarantee that I would spiritually mature and grow after getting into a relationship with you?
23. What would be the spiritual goal or purpose of our relationship? What would we and others around us and God get out of our relationship? And how did you fulfill this goal in past relationships?

24. If we got together how would you feel about having an open relationship where we sit down with mentors occasionally so that they could hold us accountable in several areas?

25. What is God's purpose in dating and marriage? Please support your answers with the Bible.

26. Does he or she show love the way Christ has called us to love?

27. How does he or she feel about committed service to God in church, community etc.?

28. What plan does he or she have to guide the younger generation to living for God?

29. Would he or she be okay if you decided to go into full time ministry or would he or she be uncomfortable about this?

REASONS FOR GETTING MARRIED

30. What is our view on marriage?
31. Why are you getting married?
32. Do you trust each other?
33. Is this the right time?
34. How can you divorce proof our marriage?
35. What is your concept of a good and Godly marriage?
36. What do we stand to gain in marriage?

PERSONAL AND FAMILY BACKGROUND CHECK

37. How well do you know each other?
38. What do you know about each other's previous relationships?
39. How do the ways you were raised differ?
40. What was your childhood like?
41. How does your family deal with conflict?
42. How does he or she treat his or her parents?
43. How does he or she relate with his or her siblings?
44. How does he or she relate with friends?
45. How do you manage conflicts with friends?
46. What type of company/friends does he or she keep?

47. How does he or she make decisions?
48. Does he or she have any person in their lives that they are accountable to?
49. How do you feel about extended family living in your home?
50. Will anything in your past affect your marriage?

LIFESTYLE AND PERSONALITY

51. What do you like and dislike about each other?
52. What personal bad habits concern or worry you?
53. What is your relationship with food?
54. How do you feel towards healthy and fit lifestyle?
55. What role should friends have?
56. What role should an extended family have?
57. When do you want to start a family?
58. How many children would you like to have?
59. How would you feel, if we had only male or female children?
60. How will you train your children?

SEXUAL COMPATIBILITY

61. Is he or she a virgin?
62. Does it bother you if he is he is a virgin or not?
63. What is your sexual history?
64. What is your level of desire or expectations in a marriage?
65. Is your love enough to sustain you?
66. If I wanted to pursue a 100 percent hands-off relationship, what would you think of that?
67. How do you feel about Public display of affection?
68. Love or money, which is more important to you and why?

DREAMS, VISION AND GOALS

69. What are your career goals?
70. What is your vision?

71. What are your hopes and dreams?
72. What are your future plans?
73. What is he or she's attitude towards money?
74. How will you manage your debt?
75. What is your philosophy on joint bank accounts?
76. Are you a saver or a spender?
77. What areas do I need to grow and mature in and how would you build me up in those areas?

TALK TO ME

78. Are you a good listener?
79. How do you like to show affection?
80. What is your love language?
81. What are your hot buttons?
82. How do you handle conflicts?
83. Is he or she proud?
84. Is he or she passive, domineering, manipulative or firm?
85. Is he or she teachable?
86. Do we respect each other?
87. Do we bring out the best from each other?
88. Do we trust each other?
89. Are we each other's best friend?
90. Does he or she get angered quickly?
91. How do we communicate?
92. How would you be able to tell I was idolizing the relationship and how would you get me back on track?
93. If one day I woke up and wasn't physically attractive would you still love me?
94. What would be your reaction to indecent dressing?
95. Is he or she patient?
96. Is he or she a jealous person?
97. Is he or she kind?
98. Does he or she express goodness out of his or her life intentionally?
99. Is he or she joyful?

100. Is he or she faithful in little things?
101. Is he or she peaceful?
102. Is he or she gentle both inwardly and outwardly?
103. Does he or she have self-control?
104. How do you feel about late nigh outs?
105. How do you feel about taking vacations?

These questions are not in any way exhaustive and do not in any way guarantee a perfect relationship or marriage, but they definitely bring a sense of purpose and clarity to a relationship.

It is important to understand that your marriage can only be as good as your singleness. This is because everything you are as a single person completely is what you will bring to the altar and to the life of another person, so you want to be sure to come right. Stop thinking about the marriage and start thinking about you, what you are and how you can fulfil purpose.

Do Not Ignore the Signs. Now I love the way the New Living Translation explains the tree and its fruits in *Matthew 7:16-20*. It says

"You can identify them by their fruit, that is, by the way, they act. Can you pick grapes from thorn-bushes or figs from thistles?; A good tree produces good fruit, and a bad tree produces bad fruit; A good tree can't produce bad fruit, and a bad tree can't produce good fruit; So, every tree that does not produce good fruit is chopped down and thrown into the fire; Yes, just as you can identify a tree by its fruit, so you can identify people by their actions".

Therefore, no matter how much you prune, decorate and water a bad tree, it can never produce good fruit, and neither can it become a good tree. The Bible says by their fruits you shall know them. Asking the right questions before dating and during courtship gives you the power, by placing you in the right position to decipher what kind of fruits he or she produces and whether those fruits are sweet, sour, bitter, spoilt or just out rightly bad.

Marriage is often likened to an omelette; it is only as good as the eggs. If you use one bad egg and one good egg, the omelette will turn out bad as the bad egg will ultimately contaminate the good egg thereby rendering the omelette bad. The eggs can be likened to each single individual. One good individual cannot change the stain or bad smell of another individual; instead, the bad smell of the individual will make the good individual equally bad if the two walk together.

Likewise, the two single individuals can also be likened to a basket with holes and a basket without holes. No matter how much water is poured into a basket with holes, the basket will always leak, and progress will never be recorded.

In other words, be the kind of person you seek to attract. When you are single, work and develop the necessary traits as discussed in the earlier chapters of this book in other to be able to richly enjoy the blessings of being in a purposeful relationship that leads to a joyful and fulfilling marriage.

REFLECTIONS

CHAPTER EIGHT

PRINCIPLED DATING. HOW TO DATE (INTENTIONALLY) WITH A PURPOSE

"When you're surrounded by people who share a passionate commitment around a common purpose, anything is possible".

— Howard Schultz

Having read the preceding chapters, I am sure you are already wondering how to date with purpose and how to build intentional relationships. There are a million and one ways to do this, but for this book and from the context of the Christian journey, I have discussed five major and fundamental ways to date with a purpose.

HOW TO DATE WITH A PURPOSE

1. Have a list of deal breakers and do not compromise on them.

This point cannot be over emphasized. A deal breaker is 'the catch' that you cannot overlook or get over, and ultimately outweighs any redeeming quality someone may possess. Deal breakers can be discovered through critical questions, boundaries, and checks and balances in order to have a Godly and intentional relationship. If you have no idea what values are important to you, then it would be difficult to identify what values are of importance and you might most likely settle for a value that's not even meant to be on your radar. So maybe you need to exit the road to marriage at the next off ramp, or you need to stop over at the closest gas station and decide what you want in a future spouse. It's dangerous riding on the road to marriage without an idea of where you are going, or what you need on the journey because you would most likely end up attracting and settling for a spouse with the wrong values. Bear in mind that an individual may possess primary and secondary values. Primary values, the ones most important to you and your relationship with God are probably deal breakers, while the secondary values are probably not deal breakers as such. Secondary deal breakers do not usually carry as much weight as the primary deal breakers.

Deal breakers are not to be seen as a checklist for a relationship, but it is designed to give you a framework and guide to dating with a purpose. Now, when you create this list, don't be legalistic. Don't sit someone down on the first date and interview them to make sure they meet all the qualities. Take your time. Slide your questions in conversations gradually, and skillfully tick your list off one at a time.

2. Do not ignore the signs.

Now, this has been briefly discussed in chapter four of this book and is also similar to having a list of deal breakers. However, what I did not mention was that signs are very vital. As a matter of fact, signs are the best ways to decipher someone's personality, lifestyle, values and beliefs in other for you to know if this falls within your deal breaker or not. Now, no one is perfect, so it would be a little bit too over the top if you begin to hunt out for signs and then snap at every sign that reveals itself to you. Just as you have primary and secondary deal breakers, so also should you vet the signs properly. Many at times, you find that the sign someone shows you repeatedly turn out to be who they truly are. I used the phrase 'many at times' because certain people do certain things, but that does not necessarily describe who they are. This could have been due to circumstances, peer pressure or just one of the moments they allowed the devil to steal them away and one thing led to another. It may be far-fetched to judge someone solely based on signs that have not repeatedly occurred during the relationship. Never the less, whatever signs stand out for every individual are sometimes different. Hence, do not ignore what you feel strongly stands out for you. Only you can know those signs, and if you are vigilant enough with a discerning spirit, you will observe the signs. Do not ignore the signs.

3. Date with a trajectory towards marriage.

Dating with a trajectory towards marriage is simply dating with a purpose or aiming to get married as a goal. It means dating someone who meets the values and goals you have for a future spouse. There is a focus. Casual or purposeless dating has no benefit for Christians for we are intentional beings and we ought to live intentionally. As humans, we are naturally designed to ask questions, know why we do things and where we are going. Dating is no different. Dating with a trajectory towards marriage doesn't mean you only date one person ever. That would be awesome, but it's not always realistic.

You might get into a relationship with someone who loves Jesus, meets the values you need in a future spouse, and is compatible with you. But once you get into the relationship, you may quickly realise things aren't as they seemed, maybe particular character and traits begin to manifest in the life of the person that you are not comfortable with. That's always a deal breaker. Usually, this is where a relationship deteriorates into a situation-ship. If you are however discerning, you may just end the relationship, and continue to seek the Lord.

You find that most people choose to remain in certain relationships because the deal breaker is not so necessary, or they believe that with time, the person could change, so they hang in there much longer without fulfillment. And then over the years of waiting, this person becomes a shadow of his or herself by choosing to remain in a relationship without purpose, till it becomes rather too late. Never compromise. Just end the relationship and continue to seek the Lord.

Now, ending a relationship will depend on if the deal breaker is primary or secondary. Once the primary deal breakers have been broken, such relationship train will have to pull up at the nearest station and terminate there. A deal breaker to every person would vary according to his or her plans and purpose in life. However, as Christians, we ought to have certain static deal breakers that should be adhered to strictly, except otherwise instructed by God. For instance (a) An unbeliever (b) A man or woman who does not fear the Lord (c) Someone who does not draw you closer to God (d) Someone who lives a wayward life (e) Someone you cannot grow with in the word of God and many others as the Holy Spirit lays on your heart. Many other deal breakers exist, but this will be personal to every believer. Once the deal breakers have been identified, and you are sure that they are strong enough to stand water, stick to them and do not compromise on them. Your heart and the holiness of marriage are too important to flippantly give away because you are frustrated, impatient, or settling. Be intentional.

HOW TO ESTABLISH A BIBLICAL AND REALISTIC VISION OF MARRIAGE

1. Intention.

Set goals. Goals are steps towards a desired end. Goals create a chain of priorities, inform decisions, deliberate choices and companions and determine actions. When you set a goal in dating, you indirectly take steps towards the attainment of a larger purpose.

2. Prayer.

The purpose and importance of prayer cannot be over emphasized. Prayer is simply a two-way communication with God. Whichever way you choose to communicate, either by standing, sitting, kneeling etc. prayer is very key and should not be ignored. Whether you agree or not, prayer is so essential as it holds you together in times of confusion, conflict, misunderstanding, and where you need guidance and direction. Whatever you are not sure about, whatever burdens your heart – be it in your single season or dating season – why not speak to God about it? After all, He created all things, and He knows you better than you know yourself. Commit your ways to Him and let Him be your guide.

To pray and communicate with God is to surrender all power in and of yourself to rely on His power to take charge of your circumstances. I can testify to God's faithfulness in my life and my relationships. Thankfully I learnt how to pray at a very young age, and I can say without reservation that prayer works. Worrying about your relationship changes nothing but praying about it can change everything. Don't be overwhelmed by the many ways there are to pray for your relationship and do not give place to impatience either. Seeing answers to prayers can take time, so be patient to persevere. Consider talking to God genuinely about your singleness, your relationship issues, your insecurities, your deal breakers, your emotions, your faith, your values, your dreams and other issues that affect your relationships. Be honest and trust God to direct you on what to do to have an intentional relationship. Remember it is your job to pray and it is Gods job to answer.

3. Set Standards.

If you do not stand for anything, you will fall for any and everything. This is the truth. To build an intentional relationship you must set clear standards and boundaries for yourself. Starting a relationship without standards is like going into the car dealers shop to buy a car, only problem is you don't know what car you want. The job of the car dealer is to sell you a car that matches your description. But without a description or idea, the car dealer will resort to showing you several cars, convincing you that any of them would do the job of moving you around without any hassle. So, you purchase one. A few weeks later, you discover the car is not brand new but second-hand, the car is very fragile and can suffer irreparable damage if involved in an accident and certain important features of the car don't work. This leaves you disappointed.

This is exactly what happens when you venture into a relationship without taking time to figure out what is acceptable and unacceptable. The truth is, without a standard, everything will be permissible, and everybody will be available. Your relationship should have parameters if not the relationship will set the standard for you going forward. There is nothing like a standard that is too high when it comes to being intentional about your love life. There is either a standard that is attainable or a standard that is not attainable. Set Godly standards from godly and biblical examples. When you set standards, you set a barrier between yourself and the devil, letting him know that everything about your love life will be intentional. Why leave your relationship to chance, when you can be intentional?

4. Have Christian Accountability Partners around you.

Ever heard the phrase 'never date alone'? Well, that's right. When I started dating to the age of 18, I had no one to talk to. Well, I had my parents, siblings, aunties and uncles but I was just never comfortable in discussing issues on 'boy – girl' relationship with anyone, so I always kept it to myself. This repeated itself in my dating routine repeatedly, till I decided to take a break and re-analyze my dating structure. As a young Christian dating with a purpose, it is important to have a set or group of people you trust can lift you up spiritually, physically and emotionally when you fall. They would be your accountability partners, and you all have the responsibility of encouraging each other in staying strong in dating with a purpose. I guess I didn't want myself or my 'partner' at the time to be accountable to anyone; I didn't want anyone to tell us what to do or what not to do, I just wanted to do things my way. Well, now I can say, I did get my fair share of doing things my way, but it did also make me learn how not to make such mistakes again.

When you date, allow that set of people (could be your parents, siblings, pastors, youth group, trusted friends etc.) around to speak words of guidance, knowledge, wisdom, love, understanding, peace, etc. into your relationship. Your feelings can deceive you. Your accountability partners can see inconsistencies and problems you can't because they are outside the storm. I know too many men and women in relationships who refused to listen to people around them, and their prideful arrogance resulted in a failed relationship and some a failed marriage. Don't fall into this category. I agree and understand that certain people are just not about the life of letting strangers in on their business especially their love life which ought to be private. Well, I can say if you are intentional about your relationship, you will find that it is usually a gradual process in deciding who you can and cannot share your concerns with. And when you do find that person who you can talk to, you discover that you are not just talking because you want to share your private business, but because you know the wisdom which that person can offer you in return. Find men and women you trust, and allow them to speak rightly into your relationship, lifting you up daily before God. If they are not speaking properly into your relationship, then, by all means, guard yourself. Be careful who you speak to and who speaks to you. Even when you speak to people about your concerns, the ultimate decision to act on their advice is ultimately yours. Be intentional about it.

5. The Law of Attraction.

Be the partner you are seeking. Attract the partner you want by developing yourself and living your life on purpose. Set yourself apart. Live intentionally. Improve your mind, body and soul by engaging in things that would enrich and empower your life. You will find that doing these things make you a better person to the partner you aim to attract. There is always fulfillment in growing yourself daily and attracting a like mind.

6. Set a guard on your heart.

This is not a new phrase to any individual seeking to date. *Philippians 4:7* says that 'The peace of God will guard your hearts and minds as you live in Christ Jesus'. Seeking the peace of God is very vital to be able to intentionally and purposely guard your heart. The peace of God, the comfortable sense of being reconciled to God, and having a part in his favour and the hope of the heavenly blessedness, are a greater good than can be fully expressed. This peace will keep our hearts and minds through Christ Jesus; it will keep us from sinning under troubles, and from sinking under them; keep us calm and with inward satisfaction.

To guard your heart means to value yourself, as out of the heart comes the many issues of life. Stay intentional and do not be carried away by your looks, compliments, disappointments, circumstances, etc. If you are intentional about guarding your heart, whenever you sight your heart being carried away, you will be vigilant enough to get it back and put it where it ought to be. Be jealous with your heart, because the devil is also in the business of stealing and breaking hearts.

7. Deal with the little foxes.

There is no pain without gain. As humans, there are things about our lives we may not like, and we choose to ignore, hoping that someone will be comfortable enough with it to spend the rest of their lives with you. No. If you do not deal with the little foxes in your life, those little foxes and the other person's little foxes will end up clashing, resulting in unending conflicts. These little foxes could be sexual abuse when you were young, bitterness, short temper, anger, hate, pride, fornication, a lying tongue, loneliness, unwise spending, debt, etc. Why would you want to take all these broken issues to another individual when he or she is not your God? This is why we talked earlier about seeking a relationship with God and deepening that relationship because God is in the best place to help you get rid of all those little foxes. Many times, we say we are waiting on God to send a spouse our way when the truth of the matter is that God himself is waiting for us to rid ourselves of all the weight and baggage's we carry. Only then can we be able to truly love and deal with issues in a relationship as they may arise.

8. The four Green Lights.

- **What does God's word day concerning your relationship:** God established marriage. Therefore, marriage is a good thing if you have it. However, there are boundaries relating to marriage. Marriage is not as simple as people make it seem these days only to end up in divorce barely a year after. As a Christian, if the person you intend on dating or getting married to is not a Christian or the person happens to have a questionable faith, you need to stop the race as soon as possible because it's likely that you have no business running in the first place, except God has called you specifically to that race. Before proceeding in any relationship, seek God's guidance through His word. God is not a God of confusion. If you seek earnestly and intentionally, you will find what you need to, and God will reveal to you what you ought to know about that particular issue. It just might take some time. Be intentional and be patient.

- **Are you ready for marriage:** Do you have a realistic vision of marriage? Are you aware of the responsibilities and commitment you will have to take? Do you have older married couples, maybe your parents, elders in church or family friends who you have sought guidance from regarding married life? Ask yourself these questions before proceeding to an intentional or purposeful relationship. You do not want to waste anybody's time in still trying to figure out yourself during the relationship. If, however, you have started the process of being ready for marriage, communicate this to your supposed spouse and reach an agreement on if to proceed with the relationship.

- **Do you have the approval and support of your parents:** So, if you have received a word from God regarding your relationship and you are indeed ready for marriage or working towards being ready for marriage, you also ought to seek approval and support from your parents. It would be dangerous to further a relationship into a marriage that no one knows about. You should seek for honest and Godly wisdom and opinion from your parents regarding your relationship. I agree that some parents might not be able to give Godly wisdom as they could also be selfish in giving self-centered opinions. Nonetheless, let the word of God be your guide in accepting parental approval.

- **Do you have God's peace:** This light is significant as an indicator of whether you should proceed or not. When you have the peace of God regarding an intended relationship, there would be no fear in embarking on that relationship. Then you will experience God's peace, which exceeds anything we can understand. His peace will guard your hearts and minds as you live in Christ Jesus *Philippians 4:7 (New Living Translation).*

Having understood, how to date with a purpose, here is a very short dater's prayer that you can pray every day even in your single season. You can tailor the prayer to how best it suits you, but say something to God about it and let him know you are being intentional about dating with a purpose.

THE DATER'S PRAYER:

'Dear Lord, thank you for my present season. Work out your purpose and agenda in my life. In everything I do, help me be a living sacrifice, salt and light to the earth you created. Thank you for the strength, grace and mercy you give me to conquer each passing day of this season of my life. If you bring someone into my life who submits to your will and will help me to love you more, then let that person be evident to me; let me be discerning in my spirit; let me not miss your provision. And if not, let me be content with your provision and ease at my singleness till your will be done; as I seek first the kingdom of God – Amen'.

When you date with intentionality, separate and apart from the confusion of the world on sex, dependence and cohabitation, your dating decisions will have much more clarity and certainty.

KEY BIBLE VERSE

Colossians 3: 1-10. Since you have been raised to new life with Christ, set your sights on the realities of heaven, where Christ sits in the place of honor at God's right hand. ² Think about the things of heaven, not the things of earth. ³ For you died to this life, and your real life is hidden with Christ in God. ⁴ And when Christ, who is your life, is revealed to the whole world, you will share in all his glory.

⁵ So put to death the sinful, earthly things lurking within you. Have nothing to do with sexual immorality, impurity, lust, and evil desires. Don't be greedy, for a greedy person is an idolater, worshiping the things of this world. ⁶ Because of these sins, the anger of God is coming. ⁷ You used to do these things when your life was still part of this world. ⁸ But now is the time to get rid of anger, rage, malicious behavior, slander, and dirty language. ⁹ Don't lie to each other, for you have stripped off your old sinful nature and all its wicked deeds. ¹⁰ Put on your new nature and be renewed as you learn to know your Creator and become like him.

REFLECTIONS

CHAPTER NINE

NEW ATTITUDE

"Attitude is a little thing that makes a big difference"
— Winston Churchill.

"A bad attitude is like a flat tire, if you don't change it, you'll never go anywhere"
— Anonymous.

∞

No doubt, attitude is an essential factor in searching and choosing a life partner. Not just any attitude but a Godly attitude, which involves God-centered, bible-based thinking – working to view ourselves, others, our seasons and circumstances from God's perspective. If you want to stop the random sampling and random shopping, a new attitude is needed for you to be able to date purposefully. The following are a few key ways that Godly attitudes can be expressed:

• **An Attitude of Contentment and Hopefulness in every season**

This attitude is one that recognises God's sovereignty in every season, situation and circumstance. This is an attitude that recognises God's grace, favour and mercy to be bigger than problems and situations. You should ask your intended spouse if he or she is content with where they presently are. Is he or she also hopeful that seasons will change when the time is right? Or is he or she the type to fast forward seasons and bypass opportunities as they arise? Does this person view his or her circumstances with a spirit of hopelessness, or is he or she confident of God's timing?

• **An attitude of Willing Obedience to God and Modeling Christ's Love**

An attitude of willing obedience recognises the Lordship of Jesus in every area of your life. This attitude will enable you to seek after someone of similar attitude. The person you are looking to have a relationship with must be willing and consistently looking always to submit his or her life to God. Such person must strive to model the love of Christ in every way possible. It could be in the way he or she dresses, the way he or she speaks, the way he or she behaves, the way he or she cares for people, the way he or she submits to God. You want to make sure that this person is not just living by the world's standard but according to the standard of the word of God. If this is the attitude of your intended spouse or someone you wish to date, you will notice if you eventually get married that such person may have little or no problem practising submission as a wife in the home because she already understands the attitude of willing obedience and submission to God.

Likewise, are you working to develop an obedient attitude in your own life? Are you working to model Christ's love in every area of your life? There are no perfect partners, but only partners with an attitude of obedience and love to God's word will continue to grow in physical and spiritual maturity as well as Godliness. Be intentional.

• **An Attitude of setting high Godly standards**

I remember whenever I was told of a Christian lady who had set high goals for herself regarding dating and marriage, I would laugh in my mind like 'where does she think she is, ain't nobody perfect out here'.

What I didn't understand was, she wasn't looking for perfection, she just didn't want to feel the pressure of having to settle for just anything, so she set a high standard, in case she never gets 100%, she would never actually drop below 85%.

Imagine a life without rules, regulations, laws or orders. It will be a free life full of chaos. Likewise, are our lives as Christians. We need to develop a new attitude of setting high Godly standards. Learn to cut off every opportunity for sin at its root and flee from even the slightest possibility of compromise. Define what your standards are for you and stick with them. God says in *2 Timothy 2:22* "Flee the evil desires of youth, and pursue righteousness, faith, love and peace along with those who call on the Lord with a pure heart". It is entirely unnecessary to stick around to see how much temptation you can take. Don't forget the bible also says "If you think you are standing strong, be careful not to fall" *2 Corinthians 10:12*. God might not be impressed with your ability to stand up to sin but more by your obedience when you run from such temptations.

Physical interaction encourages us to start something we are not supposed to finish, awakening desires we are not allowed to consummate, turning on passions and emotions we would have to disable. For a single person seeking an intentional and purposeful relationship, this would be the wrong train to embark on. We should not get on the train and try to drop off before the train arrives at its destination. Stay off that train. I encourage you to make Godly standards and set them high. You will never regret it. Be intentional.

- **An attitude of experiencing beauty in purity**

There is beauty in purity. This is a new attitude we must all experience. Purity does not just happen; it requires obedience to God and respecting the profound significance of physical intimacy. Now, this is the problem with society today – nobody is interested in understanding the deep spiritual and emotional significance of physical intimacy. Have you tried having a conversation with your peers about intimacy or purity before? Do you recall their reactions and possibly their thoughts and opinions on the topic? It is either they skillfully shied away from having such forbidden conversation knowing fully well they are guilty of same, or they jokingly utter statements to ridicule those who try to gain a better understanding of it. It's hardly ever a topic of discussion until the need becomes necessary.

Sexual purity means much more than not having sexual intercourse before marriage. Sexual purity is especially difficult during the engagement period because when you have declared your commitment, you will naturally want to consummate the relationship. You may even feel married at certain times. What better time to establish your relationship and build trust in one another by obeying God than on this crucial point.

Physical or sexual intimacy is much more than two bodies colliding. God designed our sexuality as a physical expression of the oneness of marriage. God guards it carefully and places many stipulations on it because He considers it extremely precious. A man and a woman who commit themselves to each other in marriage, gain the right to express themselves sexually to each other. This is because they now belong to each other in marriage. But if you are not married to someone, you have no claim on that person's body and likewise have no right to sexual intimacy. This is just as God commanded us in *Hebrews 13:4* to "Honor marriage and guard the sacredness of sexual intimacy between wife and husband".

Purity is also more than physical intimacy. Purity is a lifestyle. Choosing to be pure should not only be reflected in your physical actions but your thoughts as well. In other words, purity is shown in a hearts attitude and not only in physical attitude. Let purity be your heart's choice, let purity be a lifestyle and let purity affect everything you do in life. You can make all the agreements possible, but if you fail to make purity a hearts choice and attitude, you are likely to have wasted a piece of paper with scribblings on it. Purity is not a one-time choice; it's a daily decision. Moment by moment, day by day, we are always faced with thoughts and situations that put our purity to test. Do not wear the price tag purity just because you want to portray a certain image but deep within you, you know you don't deserve the price tag. As you read on in this chapter, you will see that I have drafted a purity covenant agreement that you can adopt. In other to ensure this piece of paper with scribblings on it makes sense to you and you abide by it, you must be intentional about it. You must choose to be intentional by making issues of purity a hearts attitude and a daily choice. This is never an easy process, but ensuring we always remain pure in our thoughts, words, actions and spirit, is a daily choice we must do intentionally.

Sex drive: Offering and declaring sex before marriage is a sin and God is not simply trying to be a killjoy, but He is only protecting you from a shallow relationship and personal gain. He is protecting you from that individual who has not your next interest at heart but for selfish reasons. He is protecting you from the unnecessary tears, regrets and setbacks. He is protecting you from shameful entanglements in the web of deceit and nakedness. He sees what you don't see when you offer and declare sex before marriage.

HOW TO MANAGE THE SEX DRIVE

1. **Define 'sex' biblically:** Sex is not just intercourse. *Ephesians 4:19* clarifies that the definition of sex includes every kind of impurity with a desire for more and more. Impurity in the eyes of God is not just intercourse but other activities we engage in using other parts of our bodies. The point is to keep sexuality in its rightful place. The point is to daily put our flesh in check, daily surrendering our flesh and submitting to the Holy Spirit. We ought to fight for purity and fidelity by focusing on discipleship knowing that our bodies belong to God. Therefore,

put your flesh in check and realise that God comes first. So, surrender and let God take over.

2. **Stay Accountable (Accountability Partners):** Most times, growing a Godly relationship with the opposite sex is never a job of only both parties. There's a saying that goes 'it takes a community to raise a child' Likewise, it sometimes takes spiritual leaders and guardians to make you accountable to your goal of sexual purity. Trusting people to guide you in your relationship shows responsibility and commitment to your values. This would usually keep both parties in check during the dating period. This is not to say that persons who have spiritual leaders never fall short of their values, most certainly, but life's journey is better when you have the help of others to prevent you from falling or help you up when you fall, than making the journey yourself. If you surround yourself with sharp irons, who have overcome certain battles in their relationships. Make no mistake; iron sharpens iron, so don't surround yourself with dull knives. *Proverbs 11:14* – Without wise leadership, a nation falls; there is safety in having many advisers. *Proverbs 12:15* – Fools think their own way is right, but the wise listen to others.

3. **Purity covenant agreement:** Couples should be able to talk about their past sexual experiences in other to know each other's weaknesses - not to be taken advantage of but to help in ensuring you both acknowledge and uphold your values. A purity covenant will act as a check and balance for couples to ensure they live up to a purpose and goal of their relationship. This can however only work if you make purity a hearts attitude as discussed above. The written purity covenant below could be adapted for couple's keen on fighting for purity.

THE PURITY COVENANT AGREEMENT

Scripture: 1 Thessalonians 4:3-8 For this is the will of God, your sanctification: that you abstain from sexual immorality; that each one of you know how to control his own body in holiness and honor, not in the passion of lust like the Gentiles who do not know God; that no one transgress and wrong his brother in this matter, because the Lord is an avenger in all these things, as we told you beforehand and solemnly warned you. For God has not called us for impurity, but in holiness. Therefore, whoever disregards this, disregards not man but God, who gives his Holy Spirit to you.

Agreement: In obedience to God's command, we promise to protect our sexual purity from this day until our honeymoon. We promise to live in holiness and in purity.

Scripture: 1 Corinthians 6:18-20 Flee from sexual immorality. Every other sin a person commits is outside the body, but the sexually immoral person sins against his own body. Or do you not know that your body is a temple of the Holy Spirit within you, whom you have from God? You are not your own, for you were bought with a price. So, glorify God in your body.

Agreement: This day, we acknowledge that our bodies belong to God and because we respect and honor each other, we commit to building up the inner person of our hearts and glorifying God with our bodies.

Scripture: Ephesians 5:5 For you may be sure of this, that everyone who is sexually immoral or impure, or who is covetous (that is, an idolater), has no inheritance in the kingdom of Christ and God.

Agreement: Because we are God's children, we commit to ensuring that with our bodies, mind, spirit and soul, we inherit the Kingdom of God.

PLEDGES

I pledge to show my love for you in ways that allow both of us to maintain a clear conscience before God and each other.

I pledge to keep my thoughts, words and actions pure before God and Man.

I pledge to God, my partner and myself, that I will keep my mind and body pure and holy till our honeymoon when we can give ourselves fully to each other.

This is my pledge of purity.

Signed: _____ **Date:** _____
Signed _____ **Date:** _____
Witnessed/affirmed by: _____
Date: _____

If you do not have a reason as to why you want to remain pure, you will most likely struggle through the journey. So, before you decide on a purity covenant agreement, ask yourself questions like why you want to remain pure, ensure that you and your partner are on the same page because one party's lack of commitment will eventually break the other's commitment. You cannot be accountable to each other if you are both struggling to practice purity. Be intentional about it.

Do you know that when you give your body to any and everyone, you create soul ties with that person? This is because sexual intimacy is not only physical but has a spiritual significance. This is what most people contend with. What is so spiritual about sexual intimacy? That act alone leaves bits and pieces of your heart, body, soul and spirit with the many people you have shared your body with physically and spiritually. Only if you have a discerning spirit will you attest to this truth. We are not aiming to win a trophy here but aiming just to do it right and be intentional about it. There is profound physical and spiritual significance to sexual intimacy. Find the beauty in staying pure, not just physically but purity in mind as well.

The attitudes shared above are pointers as to what may matter more in finding a spouse – the things we should look out for in our own lives and in the opposite sex. It would be dangerous to use these new attitudes as an excuse to avoid marriage as a totality. Mind you; everyone goes through different seasons and along the way develop the necessary things they need for the next season. In essence, everyone's situation might be different. As much as everyone's case might be different, there is no perfect spouse, and no one will possibly achieve perfection in all the areas we've discussed. However, the first step is being intentional about it.

REFLECTIONS

CHAPTER TEN

WHILE YOU WAIT

'Our willingness to wait reveals the value we place on what we are waiting for'

— Charles Stanley

'Patience is not about waiting but the ability to keep a good attitude while waiting'

— Anonymous

'No matter how long it takes, when God works, it's always worth the wait'

— Anonymous

∞

While you wait, this is the defining part of the process but not the most challenging. We'll talk about the most challenging in the final chapter of this book. Now you have an idea of your purpose on earth, and you understand that regardless of your relationship status, you are called to fulfil purpose, and that is what you should be doing. Perhaps you just understood that every circumstance and situation in your life are seasons which you need to embrace and get the good out of. These seasons are differently timed for every individual on earth. Now, what do you do with all this information in your single season, while you wait for your next season of dating with purpose and marriage?

Practice!

Someday when the season is upon us, we want to be excellent husbands and wives, mother and fathers to our children, we want to love and be loved, then you need to start practising. I don't mean start having serial relationships to practice these things, as that would defeat the purpose of this book, but you can take advantage of your responsibilities around you. If there are responsibilities you currently have, you cannot possibly ignore them and hope to somehow magically gain the strength, character, virtue, love, and excellence that would be needed in a marriage. So how can you train for this?

Ladies, If God has given you a father, a mother, a brother or a sister, you can start by trying to understand, love and respect the men and women in your lives. Likewise, you can start by learning how to be submissive to higher authority whether at home, in church, workplace or social gathering. If I cannot love and serve my father and brother today, the chances are that I would find it difficult to love and serve my husband in a marriage. You can say it is different. But ask yourself, is it really that different? Have you forgotten that whatever attitude or behavior you make a habit sticks as close as a brother and would always show itself even when you don't want it to or when you least expect?

Now, I am not saying practising love, respect, submission, etc. at home or even with friends will make marriage a bed of roses for you, no, these experiences will only act as a mirror, showing what and who we already are. Isn't it a great thing to find a Godly man who adores his mother and his sisters, no doubt he would surely adore, love and respect his wife in marriage. One of the men I dated many years ago is a prime example. He absolutely loved and adored the females in his household and even extended this to his friends too. During our 'relationship', he loved me quite alright, I did not have much problems in that area, but so many other things just did not fall in place. As a result, that relationship did not move forward although at the time, I got the love I needed while I needed it. It is important to practice now, what you want to be in the future. Let's discuss a few areas we can prepare while still in the single season.

Practice Openness: What is your relationship with family, friends and your colleagues at work like? Are your communication habits bad, just okay or great? Growing up, there were several instances where I noticed that my communication with my mum was just terrible. I would rather keep things to myself and not bother to share, and sometimes I would rather not communicate at all. It was better for me to keep it all in and once an argument or a misunderstanding ensued, I poured it all out. It was terrible. I quickly learnt over the years that such character and attitude will be unpleasant in a marriage because if I shut out the people closest to me now, I'll do the same thing one day to my husband and children and before you know it, it becomes a routine. I soon learnt to be open, share my feelings, discuss issues, and seek peaceable solution. So, instead of retreating to my room after dinner or after work, I hang around and have little chats. So many people are like this, and as much as this is not an easy process, it's definitely the right thing to do in preparing yourself as someone's spouse.

Practising openness will enable you to feel comfortable about discussing issues with your spouse, and there will be no reason to hold anything back (except a surprise of course). If things are bothering you, instead of suffering and wallowing in silence, you can share such issues with your spouse and your spouse in return will be happy that you can open up to him or her and will also be encouraged to open up to you as well. That little practice on your own benefits both lives in the marriage altogether.

Practice fellowship with others: Very important. As a Christian, your relationship with God should take priority over every other thing on earth. I'm sure this is not the easiest of things for people to do especially as singles. However, if you want to build a marriage or a home on

Christ and Godly principles, you need to not only practice fellowship but practice fellowship with others. It is sometimes challenging to coordinate your own spiritual life, but what happens when there is now two of you? Each of you must then learn to develop and grow your personal relationship with God first. This would usually involve things like personal Bible study, group Bible study, prayer sessions, meditation, intercession, service at a local church, etc.

Growing up in a Christian home, we usually had family devotion in the mornings and night time regularly, so I was quite familiar with praying and studying the word of God together. But it soon became a routine, some days I just wanted time to pass quickly, I would roll up some more on my bed before going downstairs to join the rest for devotion as I was not interested in the message. Other days I would be the first to get down for devotion, so I could lead, I was that interested. But during this process, my parents would make it compulsory for my siblings and I to always memorise some scriptures in the bible as our memory verse, and we would have to recite it the following day. This was a good exercise for me as I was able to learn and familiarise myself with a lot of scriptures, especially knowing the ones to recite at night before I go to bed.

During my first degree at University where I grew to know God more for myself, I was a worker at my local church, and I was also able to fellowship with a group of people from church. My church called this fellowship 'Cell Group'. What happens is there are about 5 -8 of you who live close to each other in a group, you pick days in the week when you would like to study the word and pray together. We did this by taking turns at each other's houses every week. It was a beautiful experience. I always looked forward to our next cell group meeting every week and always more excited when the meeting place for the week was at my apartment. I would have cooked and prepared enough food and drinks for my group, so we can eat and drink after fellowshipping together. The wisdom we did not know we had was always manifested. The Holy Spirit continually taught us every single time; we held ourselves accountable, we got to share personal stories of how God has dealt with us on different issues of obedience, humility, faithfulness, forgiveness, trust and so much more. Bible passages began to make much more meaning to me, I no longer read a scripture in passing but sought after the message it had. When I had finished at the University and had to relocate, it was a bittersweet feeling, I wished I could take my cell group members along with me, but I left them still carrying on strong with the cell group. What an awesome example of redeemed time! We not only built each other up but we also learnt how to seek God side by side. That transparency practice, openness practice and ability to fellowship with each other would surely sustain our future marriages.

Practice Parenthood: Whichever way you choose to look at it, children are one of the many blessings in a marriage. It is the joy of every man and woman to be able to be part of the creation of a baby. Have you been blessed with younger siblings, younger cousins, nephews, nieces or your friend has a child or children?

While parenting is an entirely different league from being a brother or a sister or cousin or uncle or aunty, you can still practice parenthood now by investing little time in the lives of these people. Notice I said little time and not all the time in the world because even parents are daily learning how to be the best father or mother to a child, so it isn't something you can learn at once. But starting now would prevent you from being totally oblivious of things when you get married. So, look for opportunities to practice and learn now, whether or not you have younger siblings. Every little time you give to this practice adds up to your years of experience, of which you can never have enough of the experience.

One other way you can prepare for parenthood is by observing good parents in action. This could be your parents, parents in church or parents of your friends. You would want to know how Godly dad's and mum's train their children about life, God and discipline. These are not the things taught in our schools, and as such, you would be doing well to take the extra effort in preparing yourself adequately. You would need it in your season of fatherhood or motherhood.

Practice Financial Responsibility: Growing up, not many children I knew were taught about money and the habit of saving. I had to make the conscious effort to learn not only how to make money but also how to be responsible with money. Do you engage in unwise spending, do you budget, do you save, and do you tithe consistently? Try working out a budget plan for yourself now that it is just you, and see how much you earn, how much you spend and how much you can save at the end of a month. You will either be impressed with yourself or disappointed at yourself. Whenever I tried creating a budget and mapping out my spending, I was always disappointed with myself. I had learnt how to save when I was much younger, but somewhere along the line growing up, I became more interested in so many things that were of little or no value to me, things I wanted and not necessarily needed. It wasn't a good experience.

It is important to cut back on unnecessary spending. As singles, most of us do not have as many responsibilities as married folks, so we need to be intentional about our money, making sure that we don't develop patterns with money that would jeopardise a marriage, or even waste God's resources. Try to establish a philosophy towards your finance and work with it diligently. Once you can do this, you would be able to have a more meaningful conversation with your intended spouse about finances, budgeting, spending and saving. An excellent book to guide you on money is *'Rich Dad, Poor Dad'* by Robert .T. Kiyosaki. It is a very good book for children seeking to learn or parents looking to teach their children about money.

Practice Practical Life Skills: Life skills are things needed to get us through the struggle and hassle life throws at us sometimes. These skills could include maintenance of the house, cleaning the car, learning how to cook, learning how to clean, learning how to listen more than speaking, learning how not to be easily angered, learning how to be humble, learning how not to be proud, learning how to be patient, learning how to be kind, learning how to have self-control, learning how to have conversations etc. What you will find out is that these things are not the easiest to do, but they are essential in our daily lives especially in a relationship where it is not just you involved alone.

Try identifying and listing some weak spots in your life that need attention or skills you want to learn and intentionally seek ways to make yourself better.

Can you think of a few ways to redeem your time while you wait, so that you can feel confident that you are making the most of your single season? What would you like to start practising today? Write them down and intentionally work on them.

REFLECTIONS

CHAPTER ELEVEN

WHAT NEXT? TRUST IN THE LORD

"Many are the plans in a person's heart, but it is the Lord's purpose that prevails"

(Proverbs 19:21).

Now, this is the most challenging of the process.

Do you believe that God knows best? Are you willing to trust Him through the process, every season and time of your life? In *1ˢᵗ Timothy 6:6*, Paul in the Bible tells us that "godliness with contentment is great gain". Contentment is not necessarily being satisfied or happy with a particular thing, but it is more of accepting where you are in life and making the most of where you find yourself. Now, whether you do this positively or negatively is entirely your choice. Paul further shares with us in *Philippians 4:11 & 13* that "I have learned to be content whatever the circumstances" because "I can do everything through Christ who gives me strength". Paul trusted God to give him the strength to endure any situation that he faced, and in this, he was able to find contentment.

The same goes for us; we can find contentment in every season of our lives when we trust entirely in God's strength, power, grace and mercy to see us through the entire season or circumstance. Believe it or not, whatever your relationship status is today, the key to being content in wherever you are is trust. Being content in every season of your life helps to project better for the next season, however, if you are discontent with season one (singleness), you may miss the gift of the moment, and you may most likely also find discontentment in season two (dating). The reason for this is because we define our happiness by our future, forgetting about the present.

I came across this quote, and I believe it is very apt in making use of your time in every season instead of wishing you could end a season and quickly move on to the next. Author John Fischer, speaking as a single young adult, said:

> *"God has called me to live now, not four years from now. He wants me to realise my full potential as a man right now, to be thankful for that, and to enjoy it to the fullest. I have a feeling that a single person who is always wishing he were married, will probably get married, discover all that is involved, and wish he were single again. He will ask himself, "Why didn't I use that time, when I didn't have so many other obligations, to serve the Lord? Why didn't I give myself totally to Him then?"*

Now, this quote reminds me of the story I shared in the second chapter of this book about the boy with the gold thread. Instead of rushing into another season of your life because you don't seem to like the current season, why not commit to using your singleness to its fullest potential, so that when that season is up for you, you can look back and be glad that you did all you did in your single season. Enjoy every opportunity that comes with singleness today before the season is up.

Let time be your friend: Time will help you see whether you and the other person are a fit or not. Time will make known any transparency, hiding, façade, integrity, falsehood, etc. Time helps get past the lies in dating. It does if you are patient enough. Time will reveal everything. Use the test of time to make sure that your significant other is not 'dancing with borrowed shoes'. Don't dismiss time. *Ephesians 4:25* - So stop telling lies, let us tell our neighbours the truth, for we are all parts of the same body'. *Ecclesiastes 3:1* - "There is a time for everything and a season for every activity under heaven…"

Notice how God says there is a season for everything in life. Not one thing, not some things, but every single thing. That suggests then that there is a season for matters related to our hearts. In other words, there is a season to wait, date and marry. Therefore, we should always be asking, "Lord, what season do you have me in right now?" Then we can embrace it, live it, honour it and learn from all God wants to teach us through it. When we are in a hurry to jump from season to season, or if we are oblivious to the season into which God is calling us, we can miss out big time on opportunities for growth, maturity and service.

I admit it myself. This was one area I often had difficulty in. When it came to relationships, sometimes I would fear that God would match me up with someone that didn't possess all the requirements I had written down or at least all the essential ones. These concerns were very baseless as I had not fully and truly understood what it meant to love. I allowed my lack of faith for certain issues to affect the way I ought to view relationships from God's perspective. I feared that if I did not commit to anyone during school, it would be harder to find someone and commit to that person in the real working class world. Because I knew I was not so much of the social type, I knew trying to find someone and being in the right social gathering, and all might prove difficult for me and may then elongate my season of singleness. So instead of trusting in His timing and trusting that however long it took, He will give me the strength to go through the season, I would often try to take things into my own hands. I would grab my life's calendar from God and pencil down my own plans and ideas just in case God forgot me. But then I see that my own plans and agendas do not necessarily work out as planned, so I eventually hand back the calendar to God to schedule my season. I mean, I trust you, Lord, it's just that sometimes I feel like I may need to help out a little.

I soon learnt that those periods when God was silent, were times used in molding me and making me better for the next season. So, if I had forcefully decided always to have my way and my agendas, I would have missed out on the molding, and my plans would have ended in disasters because it was not my time, I was certainly not ready.

A case in point was one of my previous relationships. I had been so certain that as I was leaving school, someone was going to approach me with a serious commitment. I really was not on the lookout for that someone but that someone found me somehow. As you would imagine, I was too sure it was God, so I didn't bother speaking to God about it till I was a few weeks into the relationship. Then I started talking to God, just to make sure we were still good. The relationship was so rosy; I felt it was really God, but about nine months down the line, the tables were turned, it wasn't as rosy anymore. Then I began to talk to God even more, and He wanted me to detach myself from that relationship. It was a toxic one. I wasn't ready to separate myself, so I held on for another nine months before I finally gave up. This experience made me understand that I really was not ready for what I signed up for, I went ahead of God on this one, and he left me in it for that period to learn some vital lessons from it, which I did. I must have had my own life calendar all the while. After the breakup, I was sure I did not know how to choose a man, so I gave the calendar back and asked God to help me choose. I guess God did not need my little help after all.

Guess what? A few months after handing my life's calendar back to God, I was busy minding my business in active service at my local church, not being concerned about the next relationship or anything of that sort and God led my husband to me. He found me. Yes, he did. It happened in the most unusual way – at least not in the way I would have planned it if I was in control. I had just moved (reluctantly) into a new apartment on a different side of the city. I say reluctantly because it was going to cost me more money to be there, than if I had stayed with my cousin at the far end of the city. I wanted to be close to my University campus, so I moved. I was taking a walk one evening and about five minutes later, I discovered a church just down my street and I remember saying to myself 'perfect, this is going to be my local church'. My husband lived about two hours away from that area but happened to be attending the same church I had just found. He was that committed. He was intentional.

There was no doubt in our minds that our meeting was surely orchestrated by God. It couldn't have been otherwise. We were both in active service in our local church when we met. We grew from friendship, prayerfully into an intentional dating relationship and eventually into marriage. The more we both grew together, the clearer it was to me why my previous relationships never worked out. I remember crying out to God, pouring all my heart aches unto Him, I just wanted to be rid of all the baggage I was carrying, I just wanted a renewed strength to start afresh. I trusted God just as I obeyed Him to leave my previous relationship. It was hard. It was difficult. But, it was totally worth it. After several purposeless relationships, today, I am married to my absolute best friend, a man who constantly makes me thankful that I did not settle for less, a man who loves me like Christ loves the church, a man who is committed to a life time of intentional living with me side by side. We have since been intentional with our relationship.

Learning to trust God in our seasons is one of the best things that can happen to us because He said it Himself "For I know the plans I have for you, plans to prosper you and not to harm you, plans to give you hope and a future" *Jeremiah 29:11*. So if God has said something concerning your life, regardless of your relationship status trust Him and be content in your season. He certainly sees what you cannot see, and He knows better than you. He will not leave you nor will He forsake you. You just need to ask for the strength necessary for each day of every journey and season of life.

Remember, marriage itself is also a season. It is not the last season of life, neither is it the finish line. So, we will still need to trust God even when the seasons change. So, start now.

After all said and done, remember you will be intentionally committing to sharing your lives forever, hence marriage is an intentional leap of faith, and there are no guarantees. Build intentional relationships. Be intentional.

REFLECTIONS

Printed in the United States
By Bookmasters